AN ACT OF **GOD**?

Answers to tough
questions about God's
role in natural disasters

Tyndale House Publishers, Inc.
Carol Stream, Illinois

ERWIN W. LUTZER

Visit Tyndale online at www.tyndale.com.

TYNDALE and Tyndale's quill logo are registered trademarks of Tyndale House Publishers, Inc.

An Act of God?: Answers to Tough Questions about God's Role in Natural Disasters

Copyright © 2011 by Erwin W. Lutzer. All rights reserved.

Previously published as *Where Was God?: Answers to Tough Questions about God and Natural Disasters* under ISBN 978-1-4143-1144-9.

Cover photo copyright © Nick Tzolov/iStockphoto. All rights reserved.

Designed by Alberto C. Navata Jr.

Unless otherwise indicated, all Scripture quotations are taken from the *Holy Bible*, New Living Translation, copyright © 1996, 2004, 2007 by Tyndale House Foundation. Used by permission of Tyndale House Publishers, Inc., Carol Stream, Illinois 60188. All rights reserved.

Scripture quotations marked NIV are taken from the Holy Bible, *New International Version,*® *NIV.*® Copyright © 1973, 1978, 1984, 2011 by Biblica, Inc.™ Used by permission of Zondervan. All rights reserved worldwide. www.zondervan.com.

Scripture quotations marked NASB are taken from the New American Standard Bible,® copyright © 1960, 1962, 1963, 1968, 1971, 1972, 1973, 1975, 1977, 1995 by The Lockman Foundation. Used by permission.

Scripture quotations marked KJV are taken from the *Holy Bible*, King James Version.

Library of Congress Cataloging-in-Publication Data

Lutzer, Erwin W.
  An act of God? : answers to tough questions about God's role in natural disasters / Erwin W. Lutzer.
     p. cm.
  Rev. ed. of: Where was God?
  Includes bibliographical references.
  ISBN 978-1-4143-6494-0 (sc)
1. Natural disasters—Religious aspects—Christianity. I. Lutzer, Erwin W. Where was God? II. Title.
  BT161.L88 2011
  231´.8—dc23   2011036601

Repackage first published in 2011 under ISBN 978-1-4143-6494-0.

Printed in the United States of America

17 16 15 14 13 12 11
 7   6   5   4   3   2   1

For R. C. Sproul, a friend who never tires of reminding us that God is sovereign both in history and in nature and that our trust in Him is well placed.

\\\

God is our refuge and strength,
an ever-present help in trouble.
Therefore we will not fear, though the earth give way
and the mountains fall into the heart of the sea,
though its waters roar and foam
and the mountains quake with their surging. . . .
"Be still, and know that I am God;
I will be exalted among the nations,
I will be exalted in the earth."
The LORD Almighty is with us;
the God of Jacob is our fortress.
Psalm 46:1-3, 10-11, NIV

Contents

Foreword

IN NEARLY FOUR DECADES of being an eyewitness and responder to the destruction of natural disasters—from droughts in Africa to tsunamis in Indonesia to earthquakes in Haiti—there is no question in my mind that God's heart breaks as He watches His creation suffer. For the people caught in the grip of these life-buffeting events, the losses and despair are overwhelming. I've heard the question asked over and over again in the aftermath of an "act of God"— where is God in all of this? Why didn't He do something? It's a question Erwin Lutzer examines thoroughly in the pages you're about to read.

Natural disasters have always been part of humans' lives; many examples of such harrowing experiences are recorded in the Bible. Today, for believers in the Lord Jesus Christ, these unwelcomed events can deepen our fears and derail our faith or can deepen our faith and dispel our fears. How we choose to respond depends on where our faith is placed.

So where is God when these tragedies happen? The Bible

gives us answers, but we don't always discern the fullness of the underlying truth in those answers. Dr. Lutzer does not shy away from asking the tough questions. He poses them and then points us to God's standard: for His ways are higher than our ways, and His thoughts are higher than our thoughts (Isaiah 55:8-9).

I think you'd agree that people love the beauty and calm of the ocean but loathe its raging waters driven by the fierce winds of hurricanes. People soak in the brilliance of the sun but scorn its heat that scorches the fruit of the soil. People enjoy life's pleasures but despise disease and death. We blame God for allowing bad things to happen yet we call out to Him for help in times of tragedy and loss. In the midst of our hopelessness, we pray for a ray of hope. Why can't God's creation be breathtakingly beautiful and serene every day, every place on earth? Dr. Lutzer zeroes in on a basic truth that many of us have not contemplated: "Nature is cursed because the human heart is cursed by sin."

Yes, the greatest of all natural disasters happens in the human heart . . . the disastrous result of sin. God has used natural disasters since the beginning of time to bring about redemption. He brought a dreadful flood in Noah's day, destroying creation but bringing salvation to one family who believed His warning. He brought devastating famine in Joseph's day to save a nation so that they would believe He is the Sustainer of life. He brought a destructive earthquake the day Jesus Christ gave His life for us on the cross to save people from their sin. The most horrible of all events brought about God's most precious gift—His Son, our Savior. Jesus

Christ was God's provision to redeem men, women, and children from the grip of sin that hovers over human souls.

Do we really believe that storms can draw us closer to the Son? Can they deepen our faith in the One who overshadows the darkness? Is it possible to draw from His strength and overcome? While Scripture does not provide the details as to why God allows and even brings about tragic events, we are to pray for discernment on how to respond as we seek to glorify Him regardless of tumultuous circumstances. He wants us to focus our plea for deliverance on Him. In doing so, those who don't know Him will marvel at the *Source* of our dependence.

What good can come from natural disasters? Many would say "nothing." Yet I have seen multitudes thank the Lord for life's storms because they ran to Christ for salvation. In his book *Storm Warning*, my father writes, "Benevolent hands reach down from heaven to offer us the most hopeful warning and remedy, 'Prepare to meet thy God.'" I believe this is at the heart of what you are about to read. Storms and other natural disasters that disrupt our world are God's megaphone sounding the warning, "Prepare to meet thy God," followed by the most hopeful message for the soul, "Don't let your hearts be troubled. Trust in God, and trust also in me" (John 14:1).

When the roll of thunder makes our hearts pound, when tidal waves flood our minds with fear, when winds threaten to carry us away in hopelessness, trust in Him. Don't blame God for the storms of fallen nature; look for Him in the midst of the storm. Take hold of the One who "has His way in the whirlwind and in the storm, [for] the clouds are the dust of His feet" (Nahum 1:3, NKJV). It is by His strength that we can walk through the rubble of life's storms, reaching for the hands of the fallen and touching the hearts of those who have lost faith. We can take hold of the promises from the One who gives comfort to those who recognize that their need can only be satisfied in God.

Franklin Graham
President and CEO
Samaritan's Purse
Billy Graham Evangelistic Association

Introduction
A HEART FOR THE HURTING

He heals the brokenhearted and bandages their wounds.

PSALM 147:3

LIKE YOU, I was overwhelmed by the images on my television screen of decimated villages and despairing people in Japan in the spring of 2011. Most of you vividly remember the horrifying news and the staggering before-and-after pictures in the wake of the earthquake and tsunami that hit the island nation on March 11, 2011. Entire villages disappeared. Boats, trains, and airplanes were tossed about like toys in the rush of ocean water. Weeping people searched for family and friends, even as they settled into shelters and tried to figure out where they would go next, since home was now—literally and completely—washed away.

Four months after the tragedy, the death toll in Japan had reached 15,605, with nearly 5,000 known people still missing, and at the time of this writing, there is still concern about crippled nuclear power plants. The number of the dead may never be completely known. Missing people were probably dragged out to sea. It is heartbreaking.

In 2006, when I decided to write the original version

of this book titled *Where Was God?*, I had been watching news coverage of another disaster—a CNN special report on children who survived the deadly earthquake in India and Pakistan on October 8, 2005. My heart ached as I watched volunteers helping the frightened youngsters. Those children—most of them newly orphaned—were bandaged and bruised. Some had eyes swollen shut, while others sat silently, their vacant faces revealing the shock they had experienced. Volunteers were doing what they could to provide comfort and basic necessities to the survivors. But many people trapped in remote villages had no help whatsoever. Eighty thousand people died in that 2005 quake.

Sadly, such disasters are not all that unusual. The October 2005 earthquake in India and Pakistan hit less than a year after one of the largest natural disasters in modern history, the tsunami that swept through Sri Lanka, Thailand, India, and a number of other countries in December 2004. The death toll following that disaster was almost 230,000 people. Think of it! The average football stadium has about fifty thousand seats. We're talking about almost five football stadiums full of people! The number is almost unfathomable—and many of those people were lost within minutes of that massive tsunami crashing into the coastlines of the countries in its path. A year after the tsunami, two million people were still homeless and many of them had hardly even begun to put their lives back together. Who can measure the number of tears wept because of disasters like this?

Those of us who live in the United States vividly remember Hurricane Katrina, which washed away much of the Gulf

Coast in August 2005 and nearly destroyed the city of New Orleans. Pictures of the thousands of people gathering aimlessly around the Louisiana Superdome—set up as a temporary shelter for about twenty thousand survivors—are etched in our minds. Every survivor has his or her own horrifying story to tell: A mother screamed out to her child as he was swept away in the rising waters. A family huddled in their attic and waved frantically for rescuers. In all, more than a thousand people died, and hundreds of thousands were left behind to try to regain some kind of normalcy.

I cannot help but ask myself, *What kind of a God allows such disasters to happen?*

And they happen over and over. In all, the 2005 hurricane season was the most active in history: twenty-seven tropical storms (including fourteen hurricanes) were named. But the devastation in lesser-known disasters is just as terrible for individual families and children. Tragedies kill and destroy every day, though only the large-scale events make the news. In late April 2011, tornadoes ravaged the southern part of the United States, taking out entire cities—killing men, women, and children. And a month later, Joplin, Missouri, took a direct hit from a multiple-vortex EF5 tornado that claimed 160 lives, making it the country's deadliest single tornado in more than six decades.

I believe God is real, and I love and trust my Lord and Savior Jesus Christ. But the question still plagues me, as I'm sure it does you if you have picked up this book: what kind of God allows such disasters to happen?

Dealing with the Big Questions

Some people think we should not even ask the question about what natural disasters say about God, that the question itself is too big, for it focuses on trying to explain a "natural" event in spiritual terms. They believe that these disasters are of such gigantic proportions that there could not possibly be any hidden meaning in them, nor can anything positive or helpful be said about them.

I believe that we *must* ask the big questions—but I'm warning you now that there are no easy answers. In addition, I am well aware that little can be said to ease the pain of those who mourn the loss of loved ones. Parents will hardly be comforted when a Christian tells them that God has some hidden purpose in the loss of their child. A child who has just learned that his parents died in the collapsed house behind him would not be reassured with the words that God really does care and that He did this for some better end.

Such glib statements are not helpful and are, in fact, hurtful. Sometimes we just need to sit beside those who grieve, letting them know we care. In those moments of shock and grief, our silence along with our caring presence is far more soothing than us chattering about God's promises and purposes. I've found that it's often better to say nothing than to say something that appears to trivialize the horror. There is a grief that is too deep for words, too deep for explanations, and yes, even too deep for human comfort. Some suffering is so big and so deep that it seems impossible to believe that there is any kind of reason for it, that any kind of good can come from it, that any kind of loving God is behind it. In the end, it's better to simply give no answer than to give an inadequate or trivial one.

I'd like you to keep in mind as you read this book that although I use the term *natural evil*, I am making a distinction between natural disasters (things that happen in creation—what I've been talking about so far) and the evil things people do to each other, which can be traced back to choices people make (such as murder, injustice, war, stealing, etc.). Both types of evil are tragedies, of course, but for the purposes of this book, I want to look at natural evil, natural disasters.

In addition, it's important to remember that we only see something as a "disaster," as "evil," when it hurts us or our fellow human beings. A tsunami in the middle of an ocean that never reaches land or hurts anyone is not considered to be evil. We call it evil only when we see the devastation it brings and the people it hurts. It becomes evil because we regard suffering and death as evil.

So, "what kind of a God allows such disasters to happen?" We wonder how horrific disasters are compatible with the God who has revealed Himself in the Bible. Natural disasters challenge the limits of our faith in a good and caring God. How can we watch the news coverage of orphaned children and have our faith remain intact?

Centuries ago, Asaph, who wrote many of the psalms in the Bible, found his faith slipping when he saw wicked people prosper over godly people. He begins with an optimistic statement and then reveals his doubts:

Truly God is good to Israel, to those whose hearts
are pure. But as for me, I almost lost my footing.
My feet were slipping, and I was almost gone. For
I envied the proud when I saw them prosper despite
their wickedness.

PSALM 73:1-3

Asaph's problem was not a natural disaster, but even so,
he found it difficult to reconcile the existence of a good, all-
powerful God with the continuing injustice of the world.
Who of us has not wondered at the seeming indifference of
God toward this planet with its woes, its injustices, and its
suffering? In the face of indescribable human grief, God's
silence is deafening.

One newsman, commenting on Hurricane Katrina, spoke
for many when he said, "If this world is the product of intelligent design, then the designer has some explaining to do."
Of course, many of us believe that the Designer does *not*
owe us an explanation—yet if we believe He has revealed
Himself through the Scriptures, we are permitted to have
some insight into His ways and purposes in the world.

I have very little to say to those who have angrily made
up their minds against the Almighty—except to make this
point: when atheists ask why God would permit these evils,
they are actually assuming the existence of God. If God does
not exist, we can't call anything evil—not the disasters occurring in nature or the criminal acts of human beings. In an
impersonal, atheistic world, whatever is, just *is*. No moral
judgments are possible. I'll return to this point in chapter 4.

Ultimately, it comes around to a question of faith. Those who know God believe He has a justifiable reason for human tragedy; others treat such faith with contempt.

My Goals for This Book

I have written this book with several goals in mind.

First, we should find out what the Bible has to say about the relationship between God and natural disasters. Such a study can either turn people away from God or cause them to worship Him with even more focus and awe. My goal is to provide assurance that the God of the Bible can be trusted. His promises to those who believe are worthy of our faith and form the basis of our hope.

We'll be answering questions such as:

- Should natural disasters be called acts of God?
- Is God's involvement in such tragedies direct or remote?
- Why should we believe that God is even interested in what happens in His world?
- Did people in the Bible experience disasters? And if so, did they continue to believe in God?

It comes down to this: in light of the suffering that seems so unnecessary in this world, can we still confidently trust in God? Should we even trust a God who allows disasters that He could keep from happening?

My intention is not to pry into God's diary and pretend that I can see and understand all of His purposes; indeed, there are plenty of His purposes in these disasters that we will never know. Ultimately, only God knows why He allows disasters to occur. Rather, I want to show that *natural evil is not incompatible with the existence of a good and caring God who is in control of our world.* Together we'll encounter much mystery but, hopefully, also much insight that will guide us even as we grieve over the sorrow and suffering in our world.

Second, I want to warn against the well-intentioned but foolish interpretations that are frequently offered when disasters come. People of all faiths, including Christians, are often far too ready to read into disastrous events whatever they want to see. We must *caution against the comments of sincere people who are quite convinced that they alone have an understanding of God's mind in these matters.* In clarifying these issues, we'll take a look at the differences between the function of natural disasters in the Old Testament and those of today. If we do not make this necessary distinction, I believe we can be led to make all kinds of judgments about disasters that are invalid and even harmful.

Finally, I have written this book in an attempt to *comfort all who doubt and suffer.* It is true that the best explanations do not immediately help those who are struggling with grief. Those who believe in the God of the Bible, however, can discover a source of strength and comfort even when answers are hard to come by.

The first part of this book (chapters 1–4) deals largely with the theological and philosophical questions about natural evil. In the second part (chapters 5–6), I write as a pastor concerned for hurting people. I'll urge you to seek God in faith and keep believing no matter what tragedies come to this planet. I will also discuss our personal struggles with doubt and what to say when friends ask us about God and His relationship to the tragedies we see every day on television. The epilogue challenges us to prepare for "the big one."

As I mentioned above, for the purposes of this study, I will focus on natural evil rather than evil done by people. Clearly, God does not do the evil perpetuated in a concentration camp; human beings do. But earthquakes and hurricanes cannot be directly connected to decisions made by humans. In these tragedies, God's role is more immediate and direct.

Consequently, many Christians who might not lose their faith because of human evil find it more difficult to maintain their faith in the face of natural disasters. Even Christians wonder whether they can trust a God who allows (or causes) such disasters to occur without so much as a single word of comfort from heaven. John Keats, a nineteenth-century English poet, wrote, "Is there another life? Shall I awake and find all this a dream? There must be; we cannot be created for this sort of suffering."

There can be no doubt that this life will include suffering. But where is God in the face of such pain?

Let's find out.

QUESTIONS FOR DISCUSSION

1. Have you or a loved one ever suffered a loss due to a natural disaster? Describe what happened and how you felt.

2. In the aftermath of a natural disaster, do you tend to question God's goodness, or do you turn to Him for comfort? Why do you respond as you do?

3. How is *natural evil* different from *evil*?

4. What passages in the Bible come to mind when thinking of the struggle to believe in God's goodness in difficult times?

1
DARE WE SEARCH FOR ANSWERS?

*Everything comes from God and exists by his power
and is intended for his glory.*

ROMANS 11:36

"No, GOD! No, God! No, God!"

Those were the words of a man who apparently thought God had *something* to do with Hurricane Katrina that hit the Gulf Coast of the United States in 2005. He was one of many who prayed as he climbed into his attic to wait out the storm and the high waters. Many people who had not prayed in years (if ever) called out to God when that tragedy struck.

Fast-forward six years and listen to this report from the Associated Press on Friday, March 11, 2011, after the off-shore earthquake and resultant tsunami that rocked Japan:

For more than two terrifying, seemingly endless minutes Friday, the most powerful earthquake ever recorded in Japan shook apart homes and buildings, cracked open highways and unnerved even those who have learned to live with swaying skyscrapers. Then came a devastating tsunami that slammed into northeastern Japan and killed hundreds of people.

The violent wall of water swept away houses, cars and ships. Fires burned out of control. Power to a cooling system at a nuclear power plant was knocked out, forcing thousands to flee. A boat was caught in the vortex of a whirlpool at sea.

The death toll rose steadily throughout the day, but the true extent of the disaster was not known because roads to the worst-hit areas were washed away or blocked by debris and airports were closed. . . .

Large fishing boats and other vessels rode the high waves ashore, slamming against overpasses or scraping under them and snapping power lines along the way. A fleet of partially submerged cars bobbed in the water. Ships anchored in ports crashed against each other.

The tsunami roared over embankments, washing anything in its path inland before reversing direction and carrying the cars, homes and other debris out to sea.[1]

A marketing employee in Tokyo is quoted in the same article as saying, "I thought I was going to die."

Or think of the tornadoes that hit the southern part of

the United States during the last week of April 2011, leaving over 340 people dead across seven states, with over 250 of those deaths in Alabama alone. This tornado storm system was the deadliest since March 18, 1925, when 747 people died. An eighty-two-year-old man in Alabama said, "I give God credit" for surviving the storm, but he is struggling as he attempts to recover belongings from his destroyed home.[2]

Across many of those same states, severe tornadoes had already destroyed lives back in May 1999. Stories abounded: a two-year-old child ripped from his father's hands, thrown dozens of feet into the air before being slammed against the ground as a tornado tore through his family's home; thousands of homeless families sifting through rubble. In one instance, a huge funnel cloud skipped across the ground for four hours, killing at least forty-three people and destroying more than fifteen hundred homes and hundreds of businesses. That 1999 storm was classified EF5, the most powerful tornado there is, with winds of more than 250 miles per hour.[3] Twelve years later, another EF5 tornado decimated Joplin, Missouri, taking 160 lives.

Or consider the tsunami that hit Indonesia the day after Christmas in 2004, killing hundreds of thousands of people and inflicting terrible suffering. An earthquake in the middle of the Indian Ocean set a massive wave hurtling across the surface until it smashed into the coastline full of unsuspecting people.

Or what about earthquakes? In Haiti, a year after the earthquake that decimated the country in January 2010, there were still more than a million people living in tent cities. World Vision was working in Haiti before the earthquake, but in the aftermath, providing shelter has been the priority of the organization, a basic but critical step toward "rebuilding an entire country."[4]

How about tidal waves? Different from tsunamis, which are caused by an earthquake under the sea, tidal waves happen when the moon's gravity creates bulges on the ocean surface and the waves head to shore. When a thirty-foot tidal wave hit Papua New Guinea in 1998, it killed seven thousand people, wiping out nearly an entire generation of children.

And then there are mudslides. Catastrophic mudslides in Venezuela in December 1999 killed an estimated twenty thousand people in just a few days.

It seems that almost every day a disaster hits somewhere on our planet, with 2011 seeing the United States in the crosshairs of disasters. A record ten US weather catastrophes—blizzards, tornadoes, floods, drought, and Hurricane Irene—carried price tags of $1 billion or more each, breaking the record of nine set in 2008. Globally, with Japan's and New Zealand's earthquakes and flooding in Australia, the total was estimated at $265 billion in the first six months of 2011.[5]

So we ask a fair question: where was God?

It's a great mystery, isn't it? Why is God seemingly so silent in the presence of the human suffering we see all around us? Why doesn't He speak? Why doesn't He explain Himself? Doesn't He understand the bad press He gets from natural disasters and the human suffering they cause?

God's silence forces those of us who believe in Him to rethink our faith, cope with our doubts, and debate whether

He can be trusted. And if we can survive all that, we're still left with the responsibility of trying to explain that trust to our friends who themselves are dealing with questions. Just as earthquakes create aftershocks, natural disasters create religious aftershocks. Believers wrestle with doubts; unbelievers use disasters as justification for their refusal to believe in a loving God.

Either way, disasters force us to ask ultimate questions—yet we don't know what we'll find out. We wonder if we should even dare to search for answers.

The Earthquake That Shook Europe

We begin our discussion not with recent disasters, but rather with one that dates back to November 1, 1755. The Lisbon earthquake was probably the most far-reaching and well-known natural disaster in modern history until the earthquakes and resultant tsunamis that occurred in 2004 in Sri Lanka and in 2011 in Japan. Other disasters might have caused worse damage and more deaths, but this particular disaster in the time frame it occurred had profound ramifications on people's thinking about God.

That morning the sky was bright, calm, and beautiful, but in a moment, everything was transformed into frightening chaos. Ironically, the earthquake hit on All Saints' Day, when churches were crowded with worshipers. One would think that the people who sought shelter in a house of God might be spared. Indeed, some people even ran into the churches in the middle of 9:30 morning mass. Eyewitnesses said that people looked terrified in the chaos after the first quake.

Then a second great quake hit, and priests and parishioners inside the churches were screaming and calling out to God for mercy. But heaven didn't seem to respond to their pleas. Almost all of the churches in Lisbon were reduced to rubble, and the people hiding in them were killed.

After the initial quake, which lasted from six to ten seconds, aftershocks continued to destroy buildings and homes. Fires broke out across the city, making rescue efforts nearly impossible. This havoc was then followed by a tsunami—its high waves pounded the seaport, tearing ships from their anchors and drowning hundreds of people who had sought shelter from the earthquake along the coast. The bright morning sky was darkened with soot and dust. With earth, fire, and water combining to magnify the destruction, even cool-headed observers suspected that something—or Someone—was behind it.[6] The earthquake claimed somewhere between thirty and sixty thousand lives and reduced three-quarters of the city to rubble.

Survivors were forced to rethink many of the important issues of human existence—the ultimate questions about the purpose of life, the reason for suffering, and the place of a loving God in the middle of such devastation. News of the horror in Lisbon spread throughout Europe, and everywhere there seemed to be a whole new willingness to consider and discuss questions about life beyond the grave. Many people began to talk about building a civilization based on Christianity, reasoning that the only real hope in this life must be rooted in the next. Then, as now, people were faced with one of two choices: (1) turn against God, believing that He has no power or simply doesn't care about the plight of human beings, or (2) turn to God, believing that He has the power and plan to bring good out of the evils of this world.

As might be expected, many people clung to their faith and others sought out faith in Christ for the first time, having been frightfully reminded that their lives were in constant jeopardy and that they could die in an instant. Some historians even say that the age of revolution in France and the age of the Wesleyan revivals in England may have gained impetus from this catastrophe in Portugal.[7]

Opinions were far from unanimous as to how the event should have been interpreted. People attempted to read God's mind and, not surprisingly, came up with a variety of reasons for why the disaster had occurred.

The Danger of Trying to Interpret a Disaster

The people of Lisbon searched for meaning amid the rubble of destroyed homes and cartloads of dead bodies. Many believed the earthquake was an act of divine judgment against a sinful seaport city. A famous Jesuit (a Roman Catholic order of priests) spoke for many when he said, "Learn, O Lisbon, that the destroyers of our houses, palaces, churches and convents, the cause of death of so many people and of the flames that devoured such vast treasures are your abominable sins."[8] After all, because the quake happened on All Saints' Day, many people assumed God was saying that the sins of even His followers were so grievous that they deserved immediate judgment.

What puzzled some people, however, was that a street filled with brothels was left largely undamaged.

Against the claims of the Jesuits, the Protestants said that the earthquake was a judgment against the Jesuits who founded the city. At that time, the Inquisition was in full force, and tens of thousands of so-called heretics were being brutally murdered. Like the famous Spanish Inquisition, the Inquisition in Portugal was focused on rooting out people who had converted to Catholicism from other religions but were not adhering to the fundamental beliefs of the Catholic faith. Many such people were branded as heretics and subsequently tortured and executed.

The Jesuits responded by saying that even though over a thousand people had been determined to be heretics and were burned at the stake, the quake revealed the anger of God because the Inquisition had not done enough to root out and punish heresy.

Clearly, people were confused.

A Franciscan priest (the Franciscans are another religious order within the Roman Catholic Church) gave a different interpretation, arguing that the earthquake was a form of divine mercy. After all, he reasoned, Lisbon deserved much worse: God had every right to destroy the whole city because of its wickedness. Thus, the priest marveled at the restraint of God in allowing some people to live. God graciously did just enough to send a warning and chose to spare some in the city as an act of undeserved mercy so that people who survived could repent.[9]

Those who already believed in God accepted the general

consensus that the Lisbon tragedy had to be interpreted in light of an existence beyond earthly, human existence. They felt that God was somehow trying to communicate that there is a world beyond this one, a world that could give meaning to people's unpredictable and haphazard existence on earth. Sermons with interpretations on the lessons of the earthquake were preached for many years after.

Whenever tragedy strikes, we each have a tendency to interpret it in light of what *we* believe God is trying to say (or what we *want* Him to say). In 2004, some Muslims believed that Allah struck Southeast Asia with a tsunami at Christmastime because the season is so filled with immorality, sin, alcohol, and other excesses. And following Katrina, some Muslims said that Allah was heaping vengeance on the United States for the war in Iraq.

> *Whenever tragedy strikes, we each have a tendency to interpret it in light of what we believe God is trying to say (or what we want Him to say).*

People are still as confused about the reason for disasters today as they were after the quake that rocked Lisbon over two hundred years ago. We see in natural disasters exactly what we want to see. I'm reminded of the remark, "We know that we have created God in our own image when we are convinced that He hates all the same people we do." Disasters often become a mirror that reflects our own convictions and wishes.

All of this is a warning that we must be careful about what we say about tragedies. If we say too much we may err, thinking we can read the fine print of God's purposes. But if we say nothing, we give the impression that there is no message we can learn from calamities. I believe that God does speak through these events, but we must be cautious about thinking we know the details of His agenda. We will discuss this concept further in chapter 3.

Is This "The Best of All Possible Worlds"?

A German philosopher named Gottfried Leibniz, who lived a few decades before the Lisbon quake, was the first philosopher I know of to write a *theodicy*, a defense of God and His ways in the world. Leibniz taught that God had before Him an infinite number of possible worlds, but because God is good, He chose *this* world, planet Earth, which is "the best of all possible worlds." God ordered nature to serve the best of all possible ends. After all, a good God would do only what is both best and right.

Needless to say, after the Lisbon earthquake, people had to ask whether this was indeed "the best of all possible worlds" and whether the laws of nature were indeed ordained for the best possible ends. If God had an infinite number of worlds and chose ours as the "best," then what would the *worst* of all possible worlds look like!

Likewise, as we look around at the recent disasters that have rocked our planet, we must pause and ask, "Is this really the best of all possible worlds?" We instinctively know that it isn't—it can't be. Paradise will be the best of all possible worlds, not our current world with its suffering, corruption, and endless tragedy. No one could reasonably say this is the best of all possible worlds. If it were, then it would be "best," with no room for improvement. That is clearly not the case, and the writer of the book of Hebrews in the Bible agrees with us. The word *better* is used eleven times, and in Hebrews 11 it says that the biblical heroes longed for "a better place, a heavenly homeland" (v. 16) and that God has planned something better for His people (v. 40). Thus we work hard to make things "better" on this planet because we know this is not the best the world can be. Even in the case of natural disasters, while we are powerless to stop them from happening, we do our best to create warning systems and to minimize death and devastation. And when disasters *do* occur, people from all over the world descend upon the hard-hit areas to search for, rescue, and help suffering people. We do whatever we can to try to make it "better."

The Christian Hope

But that still doesn't help us with our core question about God's role in all of this. If this world *isn't* the best it can be, why isn't it? The Bible teaches that God created all things for His own pleasure and for His own glory: "For everything comes from him and exists by his power and is intended for his glory" (Romans 11:36). And we read that God "makes everything work out according to his plan" (Ephesians 1:11). If all things work to the glory of God and according to His plan, if indeed the details of history—along with natural and even human evil—all contribute to His eternal purpose, wouldn't it be accurate to say that even if this *isn't* the best of all possible worlds, it is being run by a God whose plan *is* the best, if only we could see it from His point of view? Does He see our tragedies through a different lens? Might there be a good and wise reason for what we see as complete chaos?

As Christians, we believe that God is able to use tragedies for the best of all possible purposes and goals. He has not allowed His creation to spin out of control; He has a reason for human pain and suffering. So, although we have to look at disasters through our eyes, we must also view them through the eyes of God as revealed in the Bible. We see events unfold in time, but God sees them from the standpoint of eternity.

Instead of looking at life from the viewpoint of a loving God who sees the end from the beginning, many believe that we are merely insects living for what amounts to a few seconds on an impersonal planet. We can never hope to understand the plans of an infinite Creator. And in some ways, they are right—but only if we reject the Bible, as they do. If we refuse to believe the Bible, we are left without promises and without hope. If we have no Word from the Creator, the world of nature is indeed a brutal and impersonal force that can reveal no hidden messages and have no ultimate reason. Left to ourselves, we could never figure out the meaning of our existence, much less the purpose in our pain.

The Reality of the Curse

But when we turn to the Bible, we are offered insight. No, not all of our questions are answered, but at least we can see that God has not overlooked the flaws on His planet. He is neither indifferent to nor unaware of what has gone wrong with nature. It is important for us to understand that there is a vast difference between the world God originally created and the one that now erupts with earthquakes, hurricanes, mudslides, tornadoes, and floods. Something is no longer right, and our world awaits the time when God will make it right. We are living on a once perfect but now flawed planet. Sin changed everything.

There is a vast difference between the world God originally created and the one that now erupts with earthquakes, hurricanes, mudslides, tornadoes, and floods.

Here is the way the apostle Paul explains it in the book of Romans:

> Yet what we suffer now is nothing compared to the glory he will reveal to us later. For all creation is waiting eagerly for that future day when God will reveal who his children really are. Against its will, all creation was subjected to God's curse. But with eager hope, the creation looks forward to the day when it will join God's children in glorious freedom from death and decay. For we know that all creation has been groaning as in the pains of childbirth right up to the present time.
>
> ROMANS 8:18-22

Paul began by saying that what we suffer now can't even begin to compare to the future glory of those who know God. Suffering is redeemable; the future will make up for the present. The last chapter has yet to be written. Answers that elude us in this life might be answered in the next.

Paul then connects the curse of nature with human sinfulness. He points out that man's state of sin was his own doing, but God subjected nature to the Curse even though it had no part in the decision: "Against its will, all creation was subjected to God's curse." Mankind, now tainted with sin, could not live in a perfect, sinless environment. So creation became an impersonal victim of Adam's personal choice to rebel.

Nature is cursed because man is cursed. Natural evil (what occurs outside of human control—what we call "natural disasters") is merely a reflection of moral evil (what occurs when human beings choose to do evil). Both are savage, ruthless, and damaging. Both can result in devastation. Yet nature is not as bad as it could be: rain is followed by sunshine, a tsunami is followed by calm, and eventually an earthquake is followed by stillness. The same is true for people. We human beings are not as evil as we could be; we are a mixture of good and evil, and all too often evil takes the upper hand. Nature is therefore a mirror in which we see ourselves.

When we see the devastating results of the recent earthquake and tsunami in Japan, we should see more than creation gone amok—we should also see a picture of the evil side of human nature: powerful, heartless, and randomly cruel. In an age that is indifferent to sin, natural disasters hold up a mirror to humanity, showing us what our sin looks like to God. Sin always leaves a trail of death and destruction with ongoing, painful consequences. Both the physical world and all of humankind await a liberation that only God can bring about.

So we work hard to make this world a better place, even as we look "forward to the day when it will join God's children in glorious freedom from death and decay," as Paul wrote. We rush to the scene of a devastating earthquake in order to do what we can to help those in desperate need. We engage in a fight against nature because we are armed with the knowledge that this world is not normal; it is not what it once was. We fight disease, create early warning systems for tornadoes, build strong foundations on our buildings, and dig trenches and burn areas of brush in order to stop a raging forest fire in its tracks. We cooperate with nature when we can, and we subdue it for our benefit. In the same way, we also fight against sin in our own lives, within our nation, and within the world. We fight against the Curse wherever it is found.

Creation "is waiting eagerly" for its deliverance. The Greek word used in Romans 8:19 fittingly describes the attitude of a man who scans the horizon on a dark night searching for the first glimpse of the dawn.[10] Nature is pictured as if on tiptoes, waiting for its own release from the Curse. God will not allow redeemed people to live in an unredeemed environment and vice versa—that is, we as humans have not yet been made perfect, so as imperfect people we could not live in a perfect environment. When God's people are fully and finally redeemed, nature will follow suit. Better days lie ahead.

From our point of view, this is not the best of all possible worlds. But we also strongly affirm that God has promised to transform this present world by removing the curse of sin and bringing about an eternity of justice and righteousness. We have the possibility of such hope only if an intelligent, powerful God is behind what we see on our TV screens when a city lies in ruins.

Natural Disasters Show What We Really Believe

The Lisbon earthquake split Europe between earth and heaven.[11] On the one hand, the tragedy stimulated interest in religion, especially the Christian faith. Church attendance increased, and people were more likely to be thinking about where they would spend eternity. They became more loyal to the church and to God.

God has promised to transform this present world by removing the curse of sin and bringing about an eternity of justice and righteousness.

At the same time, however, the quake and the resulting ultimate questions spurred the development of naturalism and the growth of the secular Enlightenment or "age of reason"—terms used to describe a time period in Western Europe when a strong belief in rational thinking and science superseded religious belief.

The great philosopher Immanuel Kant wrote a book about the Lisbon disaster and concluded that earthquakes could be scientifically explained using physics and chemistry. He argued that there was no need to bring God into the discussion regarding the cause of the quake. God only needed to be brought into a discussion when things could not be explained. It was quite unnecessary to bring Him up once it was determined that a disaster occurred because nature was behaving according to various natural laws. Unfortunately, taking God out of the discussion often raises more questions as people wonder if God has any power over His creation or any care for His people.

The Lisbon quake forced people to make a decision: the heavenly minded were motivated to become more devoted to their religious commitments; the earthly minded were more inclined to explain all of life without reference to a God who interacted with the world. In other words, people made a choice to either turn to God in faith and trust or to turn away from Him in disappointment and anger. Those who turned away did so because they trusted their own opinions more than those of the Bible.

Natural disasters still have a way of dividing humanity, getting to the bottom of our values and character. They have a way of revealing our secret loves and personal convictions. In the Gospel of Matthew, Jesus told a story about a natural disaster that exposed the inner lives of two neighbors:

> Anyone who listens to my teaching and follows
> it is wise, like a person who builds a house on
> solid rock. Though the rain comes in torrents and
> the floodwaters rise and the winds beat against
> that house, it won't collapse because it is built on
> bedrock. But anyone who hears my teaching and
> doesn't obey it is foolish, like a person who builds a
> house on sand. When the rains and floods come and
> the winds beat against that house, it will collapse
> with a mighty crash.
>
> MATTHEW 7:24-27

On a beautiful, sunny afternoon, these two houses looked identical. Only the powerful wind revealed the difference between the two of them. Disasters clarify our values, challenge our faith, and reveal who we really are. If we are rooted in the promises of Jesus, we can endure. If not, we will be swept away by our own human philosophies and narrow interpretations that ultimately leave us hopeless.

To those who say God is merely an idea, a last resort in times of difficulty, natural disasters are only a further reason to *not* believe in Him and His care. But for those who have tested God by His Word and His promises, the onslaught of past disasters as well as those that are yet to come will not destroy their faith.

> *Natural disasters still have a way of getting to the bottom of our values and character, of revealing our secret loves and personal convictions.*

Proceed with Caution

This brief introduction to natural disasters serves two purposes: First, when we hear about or experience natural disasters, we must not immediately read into the events our own specific view of what God is doing. As I've said, people will always give disasters an interpretation compatible with their religion, their understanding of sin, and their own convictions of what they think God should do. But let's also not do the opposite and speak as if the Bible is silent about these matters. Let's avoid both extremes.

Second, we must realize that to ask why natural disasters happen is similar to asking why people die. Six thousand people die every hour on this planet, most of them in anguish—much like those who die in an earthquake or tidal wave. Many more children die of starvation every day than the total number of people who died when Hurricane Katrina struck the Gulf Coast. The only reason natural disasters attract our attention is that they dramatically intensify the daily occurrence of death and destruction. Like death itself, natural disasters will be with us until God transforms the earth. And as I shall explain later, the worst natural disasters still lie ahead.

You see, if natural disasters do not serve God's good ends, then we are confronted with a God who is either too weak to make evil serve higher ends or too evil to do what is good and just. Yes, there is a great danger in claiming to know too much about God's purposes. But there is also a danger in being silent, in not saying what the Bible allows us to say about these horrific events. Natural disasters do have an important message that we dare not ignore.

In the next chapter, we'll turn to the question of God's relationship to natural disasters. Are they acts of God? Should we protect God's reputation by saying that disasters are simply the result of the Curse on nature? Or should we blame the devil for these acts? And what are the implications of our answers?

QUESTIONS FOR DISCUSSION

1. Do you think God wants us to search for answers regarding His plan in natural disasters? Why or why not?

2. In what ways do you think natural disasters mirror the evil side of human nature?

3. How do natural disasters reveal our true values and character, exposing our inner lives?

4. Philosopher Immanuel Kant said that if natural disasters can be explained by natural laws, it is unnecessary to bring God into the discussion. Do you agree or disagree?

5. The frequency of natural disasters has increased significantly in the last century. In your opinion, what factors are contributing to that increase?

2

IS GOD RESPONSIBLE FOR NATURAL DISASTERS?

Why let the nations say, "Where is their God?"
Our God is in the heavens, and he does as he wishes.

PSALM 115:2-3

I'M TOLD THAT after an earthquake in California a group of ministers met for a prayer breakfast. As they discussed impassable expressways and ruined buildings, they agreed that God had very little to do with the disaster. They concluded that since the earth is under the Curse from Creation, earthquakes and other natural disasters simply happen according to laws of nature. But even after they made that conclusion, one of the ministers closed in prayer, *thanking God* for the timing of the earthquake that came at five o'clock in the morning when there were fewer people out on the roads.

So did God have anything to do with that earthquake or didn't He? How can a person conclude that God is not involved and then thank Him for His involvement? It can't be both ways.

AN ACT OF GOD?

Hurricanes, tornadoes, tsunamis, earthquakes. Our earth is not immune to disasters. So how does God fit in? Intuitively, people know God is in charge. When tragedy strikes, people call out to Him. We know that when something is outside of our control, we need to call upon a higher power for help. But if people intuitively know that God is in charge, how do we explain the heart-wrenching suffering that accompanies such disasters?

Who Is Responsible?

There's no doubt about it—natural disasters aren't very good for God's reputation. As a result, many Christians try to absolve Him of any and all responsibility for these horrific events. They want to "get Him off the hook" in order to help Him maintain His loving image. Some do this by saying that God is weak—He can't really stop these disasters from happening, but He *will* work really hard to bring something good out of them. Others try to give the devil all the blame, saying God is not involved at all in any of the bad things that happen—He's just a bystander.

Is God Weak?

Let's begin with people who try to protect God's reputation by claiming that He is unable to prevent our planet from getting pounded by one calamity after another. These folks fear that if we say God is responsible for natural disasters or that He allows them because of a higher purpose, we will drive people away from the Christian faith. "Why would people want to come to a God who would do such horrible things?" they ask.

When we glibly say that "God will bring good out of it" or that "in the end we win," it does little to comfort those who have lost loved ones or possessions in a disaster.

I agree that glib statements about suffering being part of God's plan will not immediately comfort the grieving. In fact, it probably *is* true that giving such answers without any compassion or understanding could indeed drive people away from God rather than toward Him. As Christians, we do need to be very careful what we say to those who are grieving from great loss. Sometimes it is best to remain silent, not pretending that we have the right to speak on God's behalf, but to *act* benevolently on His behalf instead. I will talk more about this later in this chapter.

To take the approach that God is weak, unable to handle the forces of nature, is to believe that God is finite. If it is true that God is not all-powerful and must deal with natural disasters as best as He can after they happen, how can a God like that be trusted? If God is helpless in the face of a hurricane, how confident can we be that He can one day subdue all evil? To believe that God is finite might get Him off the hook for natural disasters, but it also puts end-time victories in jeopardy.

The Bible does not describe a weak God, however. In fact, just the opposite. God is omnipotent—all-powerful. Consider just a sampling of Scripture that focuses on God's power over His creation:

> In the beginning God created the heavens and
> the earth.
> GENESIS 1:1

You formed the mountains by your power and
armed yourself with mighty strength. You quieted
the raging oceans with their pounding waves and
silenced the shouting of the nations.

PSALM 65:6-7

The heavens are yours, and the earth is yours;
everything in the world is yours—you created it
all. You created north and south. Mount Tabor and
Mount Hermon praise your name. Powerful is your
arm! Strong is your hand! Your right hand is lifted
high in glorious strength.

PSALM 89:11-13

Look up into the heavens. Who created all the stars?
He brings them out like an army, one after another,
calling each by its name. Because of his great power
and incomparable strength, not a single one is
missing.

ISAIAH 40:26

[Jesus] got up and rebuked the wind and waves, and
suddenly there was a great calm.

MATTHEW 8:26

For ever since the world was created, people
have seen the earth and sky. Through everything
God made, they can clearly see his invisible

qualities—his eternal power and divine nature. So they have no excuse for not knowing God.

ROMANS 1:20

It would be strange indeed if the God who created the world were unable to control it. To describe God as too weak to handle natural disasters doesn't help God's reputation, it doesn't get Him off the hook, and it isn't biblical. The answer to the question, "Is God weak?" is a resounding no! God is all-powerful and completely able to control nature.

Are Disasters the Devil's Fault?

The second way some Christians try to exempt God from involvement in natural disasters is to simply blame everything on the devil. God is not responsible for what happens, they say. He created the world and lets it run; nature is fallen, and Satan, who is the god of this world, wreaks havoc with the natural order.

Scripture clearly tells us that nature is under a curse just as people are: "The ground is cursed because of you. All your life you will struggle to scratch a living from it" (Genesis 3:17). It follows, then, that Satan might indeed be involved in natural disasters. We have an example of this in the book of Job, when God gave Satan the power to destroy Job's children. Acting under God's direction and within certain set limitations, Satan used lightning to kill the sheep and the servants and a powerful wind to kill all ten of Job's children (Job 1). Clearly the devil takes great pleasure in causing havoc and destruction. Take a moment to look at the wretched life of the demon-possessed man before Jesus commanded the legion of demons to leave him. The Gospel of Luke describes him as homeless and naked, living in a cemetery, shrieking, breaking chains and shackles, completely alone, and without hope (Luke 8:26-29). This is a snapshot of Satan's ultimate goal for living things. Here is proof, if proof is needed, that satanic powers might indeed be connected to the natural disasters that afflict our planet.

So if the devil *is* involved, does this mean that God is removed from nature? Does He really have a "hands-off policy" when it comes to disasters? Does this absolve God of responsibility? Is it all the devil's fault? Clearly the answer to all of these questions is *no*. God has not relegated calamities to His hapless archrival the devil without maintaining strict supervision and ultimate control of nature. No earthquake comes, no tornado rages, and no tsunami washes villages away but that God signs off on it.

But that conclusion creates its own set of questions . . .

So What Does It Mean That God Is in Control?

If God isn't too weak to deal with His creation, and if we cannot put all the blame on Satan, then where does that leave us? It leaves us with the fact that God is all-powerful and in control—and that applies to natural disasters.

We must think carefully at this point. We must distinguish between the *secondary* cause of disastrous events and their *ultimate* cause. The secondary cause of the lightning and the wind that killed Job's children was the power of Satan. But follow carefully: it was God who gave Satan the power to wreak the havoc. It was God who set the limits of what Satan could or could not do. In effect, God said, "Satan, you can go this far, no further. I'm setting the boundaries here." That's why Job, quite rightly, did not say that the death of his children was the devil's doing. Instead, Job said, "The LORD gave me what I had, and the LORD has taken it away. Praise the name of the LORD!" (Job 1:21, italics added).

Scientifically speaking, we know that the *secondary* cause of an earthquake is due to a fault beneath the earth's crust; the top of the earth's crust moves in one direction while the levels under the earth's crust gradually move in the opposite direction. The *secondary* causes of a tornado are unstable atmospheric conditions combined with warm, moist air. The *secondary* cause of a hurricane is a large air mass heated and fueled by the warmth of the ocean. All of these weather patterns might or might not receive their momentum from Satan, yet we can be sure that the *ultimate* cause of these events is God. He rules through intermediate causes and at times by direct intervention, but either way, He is in charge. After all, He is the Creator, the Sustainer, of all things. We sing with Isaac Watts,

God rules through intermediate causes and at times by direct intervention, but either way, He is in charge.

> *There's not a plant or flower below,*
> *But makes Thy glories known;*
> *And clouds arise, and tempests blow,*
> *By order from Thy throne.*

So what does it mean for us that God is in control, even when natural disasters occur? How do we begin to process this?

First, many theologians who agree that God is in charge of nature emphasize that God does not *decree* natural disasters but only *permits* them to happen. Understanding the difference between these words is helpful, especially since in the book of Job God permitted Satan to bring about disasters to test Job. However, keep in mind that the God who permits natural disasters to happen could choose to *not* permit them to happen. In the very act of allowing them, He demonstrates that they fall within the boundaries of His providence and will. The devil is not allowed to act beyond the boundaries God sets.

Second—and this is important—God is sometimes pictured as being in control of nature even without secondary or natural causes. When the disciples were at their wits' end, expecting to drown in a stormy sea, Christ woke up from a nap and said to the waves, "Silence! Be still!" The effect was immediate: "Suddenly the wind stopped, and there was a great calm" (Mark 4:39). Christ could have spoken similar words to the tidal wave in Papua New Guinea or the rain that triggered the mudslides in Venezuela, and they would have obeyed Him. At the word of Christ, the tsunami in Southeast Asia would have ended before it hit the coastlines. Notice how the Scriptures credit tidal waves and tsunamis to God: "The LORD's home reaches up to the heavens, while its foundation is on the earth. He draws up water from the oceans and pours it down as rain on the land. The LORD is his name!" (Amos 9:6).

Third, if the heavens declare the glory of God, if it is true that the Lord reveals His character through the positive side of nature, doesn't it make sense that the calamities of nature also reveal something about Him too? If nature is to give us a balanced picture of God, we must see His judgment, too. "The LORD does whatever pleases him throughout all heaven and earth, and on the seas and in their depths. He causes the clouds to rise over the whole earth. He sends the lightning with the rain and releases the wind from his storehouses" (Psalm 135:6-7).

We shall revisit this idea in the next chapter.

God's Signature

After the tsunami in Southeast Asia, a supposed Christian cleric was asked whether God had anything to do with the disaster. "No," he replied. "The question as to why it happened demands a *geological* answer, not a *theological* answer." Is he reading the same Bible I am? Or has he read the Bible and simply chosen not to believe it?

Who sent the Flood during the time of Noah? God said, "I am about to cover the earth with a flood that will destroy every living thing that breathes. Everything on earth will die" (Genesis 6:17). God determined the timing, the duration, and the intensity of the rain. And it happened according to His word. It would have been difficult to convince Noah that God had nothing to do with the weather, that all He could do was weep when the Flood came.

Who sent the plagues on Egypt? Who caused the sun to stand still so that Joshua could win a battle? Who first sealed the heavens and then brought rain in response to Elijah's prayer? Who sent the earthquake when the sons of Korah rebelled against Moses? This event recorded in the Bible is of special interest:

> [Moses] had hardly finished speaking the words when the ground suddenly split open beneath them. The earth opened its mouth and swallowed the men, along with their households and all their followers who were standing with them, and everything they owned. So they went down alive into the grave, along with all their belongings. The earth closed over them, and they all vanished from among the people of Israel.
>
> NUMBERS 16:31-33

Can anyone say that God is not the ultimate cause of these disasters?

In the story of Jonah, the biblical writer leaves no doubt as to who caused the storm that forced the sailors to throw the stowaway overboard. "*The LORD* hurled a powerful wind over the sea, causing a violent storm that threatened to break the ship apart" (Jonah 1:4, italics added). The sailors agonized about unloading their unwanted cargo, but we read that they "picked Jonah up and threw him into the raging sea, and the storm stopped at once!" (Jonah 1:15). It appears that the Bible is not as concerned about God's reputation as some theologians are. It puts God clearly in charge of the wind, the rain, and the calamities of the earth.

What do all these stories have in common? Notice that

God is meticulously involved. Whether an earthquake, a raging wind, or a rainstorm, the events came and left according to God's word. In addition, many of these calamities were acts of judgment by which God expressed how much He hated disobedience. In Old Testament times, these judgments generally separated godly people from wicked people (this is not the case today, as we shall see in the next chapter). However, even back then, sometimes the godly were also victims of these judgments. Job's children were killed not because they were wicked, but because God wanted to test their father.

On the other hand, we should also note that in both the Old and New Testaments God sometimes sent a natural disaster to *help* His people. During a battle when Saul's son Jonathan killed a Philistine, we read, "Then panic struck the whole [enemy] army—those in the camp and field, and those in the outposts and raiding parties—*and the ground shook. It was a panic sent by God*" (1 Samuel 14:15, NIV, italics added). And in the New Testament, an earthquake delivered Paul and Silas from prison: "Around midnight Paul and Silas were praying and singing hymns to God, and the other prisoners were listening. Suddenly, there was a massive earthquake, and the prison was shaken to its foundations. All the doors immediately flew open, and the chains of every prisoner fell off!" (Acts 16:25-26).

Both of these earthquakes had God's signature on them.

God uses nature to do His bidding. Directly or indirectly, He can cause an earthquake to happen at five in the morning. God does as He wills.

Is Our God Really Good?

If God is the ultimate cause of all things and if He does as He wills on this earth—including with nature and natural disasters—can we put the blame on Him for the evil and suffering that these disasters cause? How can God be good when He permits (or does) things that seem so destructive and hurtful to human beings? Surely if we had the power to prevent an earthquake, if we could have stopped the tsunami, we would have done so.

As I mentioned in the introduction, natural disasters are not "evil" in the usual sense of the word. If a tsunami took place in the middle of the ocean and did not affect any people, we would not think of it as evil. It's when humans are affected, and when death and suffering occur, that such disasters become "evil."

In light of what I've said, should God be blamed for such destructive disasters that create unfathomable human suffering? The word *blame* implies wrongdoing, and I don't believe such a word should ever be applied to God. But even asking if God is *responsible* for natural disasters also might not be best, since the word *responsibility* usually implies accountability, and God is accountable to no one: "Our God is in the heavens, and he does as he wishes" (Psalm 115:3).

Let's begin by agreeing that God plays by a different set of rules. If you were standing beside a swimming pool and watched a toddler fall in and did nothing to help, you could be facing a lawsuit for negligence. Yet God watches children drown—or, for that matter, starve—every day and does not intervene. He sends drought to countries in Africa, creating scarcity of food; He sends tsunamis, wiping out homes and crops.

We are obligated to keep people alive as long as possible, but if God were held to that standard, no one would ever die. Death is a part of the Curse: "You were made from dust, and to dust you will return" (Genesis 3:19). What for us would be criminal is an everyday occurrence for God.

Why the difference? God is the Creator; we are the creatures. Because God is the giver of life, He also has the right to take life. He has a long-term agenda that is much more complex than keeping people alive as long as possible. Death and destruction are a part of His plan. "'My thoughts are nothing like your thoughts,' says the LORD. 'And my ways are far beyond anything you could imagine. For just as the heavens are higher than the earth, so my ways are higher than your ways and my thoughts higher than your thoughts'" (Isaiah 55:8-9).

The philosopher John Stuart Mill wrote that natural disasters prove that God cannot be both good and all-powerful. If He were, suffering and happiness would be carefully meted out to all people, each person getting exactly what he or she deserved. Since natural disasters appear to be random, affecting both good and evil people, God therefore cannot be both good and all-powerful. Mill forgets, however, that we don't receive our final rewards and punishments in this life. Indeed, the Scriptures teach that the godly often endure the most fearful calamities. God always acts from the standpoint of eternity rather than time; His decisions are made with an infinite perspective.

Therefore, it comes down to this: we believe that God has a good and all-wise purpose for the heartrending tragedies disasters bring. Speaking of the earthquake in Turkey that took thousands of lives, pastor and author John Piper says, "[God] has hundreds of thousands of purposes, most of which will remain hidden to us until we are able to grasp them at the end of the age."[1] God has a purpose for each individual. For some, His purpose is that their days on earth end when disaster strikes; for the survivors there are other opportunities to rearrange priorities and focus on what really matters. The woman who said she lost everything but God during Hurricane Katrina probably spoke for thousands of people who turned to Him in their utter despair.

God does not delight in the suffering of humanity. He cares about the world and its people: "But you, O Lord, are a God of compassion and mercy, slow to get angry and filled with unfailing love and faithfulness" (Psalm 86:15). God does not delight in the death of the wicked but is pleased when they turn from their wicked ways (Ezekiel 18:23).

We finite beings cannot judge our infinite God. He is not obligated to tell us everything He is up to. As Paul described it, the clay has no right to tell the potter what to do (Romans 9:19-21). It is not necessary for us to know God's purposes before we bow to His authority. And the fact that we trust God even though He has not revealed the details is exactly the kind of faith that delights His heart. "It is impossible to please God without faith" (Hebrews 11:6).

In chapter 5 we shall see that this sovereign God has given us reasons to trust Him. Faith will always be necessary, but our faith has strong supports. We do not believe clever fables but rather a credible account of God's will, God's power, and God's dealings with us as found in the Bible.

Responding to the Hurting with Compassion

The God who created the laws of nature and allows them to "take their course" is the very same God who commands us to fight against these natural forces. Before the Fall, God gave Adam and Eve the mandate to rule over nature. After the Fall, that mandate continued even though the ground would yield thorns and thistles and childbearing would mean struggling with pain. The *desire* to live would become the *fight* to live.

> *The fact that we trust God even though He has not revealed the details is exactly the kind of faith that delights His heart.*

We've seen it over and over—the relentless compassion of people reaching out to help others who have been faced with calamity. People offer money, goods, services, and their time and labor to bring aid where it is most needed. Charitable giving to the American Red Cross for Haiti relief set a record for mobile-generated donations, raising seven million dollars in twenty-four hours when the Red Cross allowed people to send ten-dollar donations by text messages.[2] This is when God's glory shines through even the darkest times.

God uses nature to both bless and challenge us, to feed and instruct us. He wants us to fight against the devastation of natural disasters, even as we fight against the devil, so that we might become overcomers in this fallen world. Although nature is under God's supervision, we are invited to fight disease and plagues.

We can and should strive for better medical care and clean water and food for the starving in Third World countries. We should be willing to help those who are in distress—even at great personal risk.

Martin Luther, when asked whether Christians should help the sick and dying when the plague came to Wittenberg, said that each individual would have to answer the question for himself. He believed that the epidemic was spread by evil spirits, but added, "Nevertheless, this is God's decree and punishment to which we must patiently submit and serve our neighbor, risking our lives in this manner as St. John teaches, 'If Christ laid down his life for us, we ought to lay down our lives for the brethren' (1 John 3:16)."[3]

God uses nature to both bless and challenge us, to feed and instruct us. He wants us to fight against the devastation of natural disasters.

In recent years, the news media have carried stories of virulent flu viruses that have infected humans in epidemic proportions. Some Christians might wonder if they should help those who are sick, risking their own lives for the sake of others. Disasters such as these make Luther's comments about the Wittenberg plague very relevant. He continued:

> If it be God's will that evil come upon us and destroy us, none of our precautions will help us. Everybody

must take this to heart: first of all, if he feels bound to remain where death rages in order to serve his neighbor, let him commend himself to God and say, "Lord, I am in thy hands; thou hast kept me here; thy will be done. I am thy lowly creature. Thou canst kill me or preserve me in the pestilence in the same way as if I were in fire, water, drought or any other danger."[4]

Yes, the plague was "God's decree," but we also must do what we can to save the lives of the sick and minister to the dying. We should thank God when He gives us the opportunity to rescue the wounded when a disaster strikes. Tragedies give us the opportunity to serve the living and comfort the dying all around us. Through the tragedies of others, we have the opportunity to leave our comfortable lifestyles and enter the suffering of the world.

Historically, the church has always responded to tragedies with sacrifice and courage. During the third century, the writer Tertullian recorded that when pagans deserted their nearest relatives in the plague, Christians stayed and ministered to the sick.

When Hurricane Katrina hit the Gulf Coast, churches rose to the occasion to help the victims. Church members prepared tens of thousands of meals for people left homeless and scattered in shelters. One church would help another begin the painful process of relocation and reconstruction. Even the secular press had to admit that governmental red tape did not stop the churches from sacrificially helping in time of need. What the government and the Red Cross could not do, the people of God did. This is how it should be. This is how we become Jesus' hands and feet in the world.

In the days after the 2011 Joplin tornado, one pastor's wife wrote to a friend, "It [the tornado and its aftermath] has certainly stretched us. All the things that pastors deal with on a day-to-day basis—marriages in crisis, pettiness, misunderstandings, sins of all varieties—do not go away when the storms come. They do not get put on the back burner. They catch fire. Other things that pastors deal with on a day-to-day basis—tireless, selfless, tenderhearted servants who are constantly seeking to please God and serve His church—do not go away either. They catch fire. I am amazed at these people."

Jesus was touched by the plight that the curse of sin brought to this world. We see Him weep at the tomb of Lazarus, and we hear His groans. "Jesus, once more deeply moved, came to the tomb. It was a cave with a stone laid across the entrance" (John 11:38, NIV). After the stone was removed, Jesus shouted, "Lazarus, come out!" (v. 43) and the dead man came to life in the presence of the astonished onlookers. The Jesus who stayed away for a few extra days so Lazarus would die is the very same Jesus who raised him from the dead.

Like Jesus, we mourn for the horrendous pain people experience on this planet. Like the weeping prophet Jeremiah, we find ourselves saying, "Rise during the night and cry out. Pour out your hearts like water to the Lord. Lift up your hands to him in prayer, pleading for your children, for in every street they are faint with hunger" (Lamentations 2:19).

Although modern medicine and technology allow us to stave off death as long as possible, eventually we will all be overcome by its power. Yet in the end, we win! Christ has conquered death.

Responding to God in Faith

If there is still some doubt in your mind that ultimately God has control of nature, let me ask you: Have you ever prayed for beautiful weather for a wedding? Have you ever prayed for rain at a time of drought? Have you ever asked God to protect you during a severe storm? Many people who claim God has no control over the weather change their minds when a funnel cloud comes toward them. The moment we call out to Him in desperate prayer, we are admitting that He is in charge.

It is also vital to understand that if nature is out of God's hands, then we are also out of God's hands. We would be nothing more than victims of nature and thus die apart from His will. Jesus, however, assures His children that He will take care of us. "What is the price of five sparrows—two copper coins? Yet God does not forget a single one of them. And the very hairs on your head are all numbered. So don't be afraid; you are more valuable to God than a whole flock of sparrows" (Luke 12:6-7). The God who cares for the tiny sparrows and counts the hairs on our heads is in charge of nature.

Have you ever asked God to protect you during a severe storm? The moment we call out to Him in desperate prayer, we are admitting that He is in charge.

The ministers in California were right in thanking God that the earthquake came early in the morning when there was little traffic on the expressways. They were wrong,

however, for saying that God was not in charge of the tragedy. Of course He was—both biblically and logically.

There is, perhaps, no greater mystery than human suffering,
so let us humbly admit that we can't determine God's ways.

The eighteenth-century English poet William Cowper
put the mysteries of God in perspective:

> God moves in a mysterious way
> His wonders to perform;
> He plants His footsteps in the sea,
> And rides upon the storm.
>
> Deep in unfathomable mines
> Of never-failing skill
> He treasures up His bright designs,
> And works His sovereign will.
>
> Ye fearful saints, fresh courage take;
> The clouds ye so much dread
> Are big with mercy, and shall break
> In blessing on your head.
>
> Judge not the Lord by feeble sense,
> But trust Him for His grace;
> Behind a frowning providence
> He hides a smiling face.
>
> His purposes will ripen fast,
> Unfolding every hour;
> The bud may have a bitter taste,
> But sweet will be the flower.

Blind unbelief is sure to err,
And scan His work in vain;
God is His own interpreter,
And He will make it plain.[5]

"Grieve not because thou understandest not life's mystery," wrote a wise man. "Behind the veil is concealed many a delight."[6]

The trusting believer knows this is so.

QUESTIONS FOR DISCUSSION

1. Does the idea of a God who "weeps" give you comfort? What are the negative implications of believing in such a God?

2. What is the difference between secondary causes and ultimate causes? How do you see this played out in natural disasters?

3. Do you believe that God could use a natural disaster for good? Why or why not?

4. List several ways in which God is different from us—both in His person and His purposes for us and the world.

5. Have you ever been a part of a relief effort, either helping on-site at a local disaster or volunteering to help in a global disaster? How did that affect you?

3

ARE THERE LESSONS TO BE LEARNED FROM DISASTERS?

No, and I tell you again that unless you repent,
you will perish, too.

LUKE 13:5

WHEN DISASTERS HAPPEN, we naturally want to understand why—and the only Person who will possibly be able to explain *why* is God Himself. But therein lies the problem: Can we, mere human beings, expect to be able to discern the purposes of the Almighty when horrible things happen in our world? Can we expect to know the lessons to be learned? We must be very cautious. We must not say too much, pretending to know more than we can possibly know, but we must also refrain from the opposite mistake of saying nothing at all.

I must emphasize that when I refer to "lessons to be learned" from natural disasters, I'm not implying that I or anyone else can figure out all of God's reasons for allowing devastations to happen. Ultimately, only He knows, and He has not seen fit to reveal the details to us. I also don't want to imply that understanding God's "lessons" in a disaster will immediately comfort those who are suffering grief and loss. In fact, let's candidly admit that *even if we knew all the reasons God sent a disaster, it would not lessen the suffering of those who have experienced loss.*

However, just because we can't expect to understand God's mind and plans regarding the reasons behind disasters doesn't mean they are completely without purpose. That's what I meant when I said above that while we ought not speak too much and pretend to understand what we cannot, neither should we be silent as if God were not involved at all.

Disasters Happen Randomly

Through His Word, God has given us a glimpse into His purposes in disasters. I think that Jesus shed some light on the question of human tragedy when He referred to the deaths of eighteen people who died when a tower collapsed on them. That tragedy was obviously on the minds of everyone in the city of Jerusalem at that time.

It is quite possible that this tower was an aqueduct built by Romans who had hired Jews to help with the construction. Of course, the Jewish zealots would have disapproved of Jewish workers helping with a project that would benefit their despised oppressors. We can imagine their response: "Those men deserved to die! God was judging them for working with the enemy!" I'm sure the self-righteous pointed fingers in those days too.

But Jesus gave a different interpretation of the event: "What about the eighteen people who died when the tower in Siloam fell on them? Were they the worst sinners in Jerusalem? No, and I tell you again that unless you repent, you will perish, too" (Luke 13:4-5). Jesus used the incident to point out that disasters do not separate the wicked from the righteous. Those who died were not greater sinners than the rest of the people in Jerusalem who were still alive. Jesus pointed out that it was both morally wrong and self-righteous to sit in judgment on those who were killed so unexpectedly.

The same is true today. It is obvious to us that disasters don't take the evil people and leave the godly ones—in fact, we wouldn't need this book if that were the case. Our problem arises because disasters cause such great suffering for even some of the most innocent among us—like the orphaned chil-

From God's standpoint, disasters might be meticulously planned; however, from our perspective they occur haphazardly and affect everyone who happens to be in the way.

dren who so touched my heart after the earthquake in India and Pakistan. From God's standpoint, disasters might be meticulously planned and have reasons beyond our understanding; however, from our perspective they occur haphazardly, randomly, and they affect everyone who happens to be in the way. Therefore, we must be very careful not to point to certain people who have been hurt or killed in a disaster and claim some kind of judgment from God upon them.

In Old Testament times, God ruled the Jewish nation directly, so He dealt with them as a group that lived within a certain geographical area. Thus there was often (although not always) a direct cause-and-effect relationship between their obedience and the cooperation of natural forces. God said He would use nature to reward or punish the people. "At times I might shut up the heavens so that no rain falls, or command grasshoppers to devour your crops, or send plagues among you. Then if my people who are called by my name will humble themselves and pray and seek my face and turn from their wicked ways, I will hear from heaven and will forgive their sins and restore their land" (2 Chronicles 7:13-14). Grasshoppers and plagues as a punishment for disobedience; rain and good crops as a reward for obedience.

Contrast this with today, when good crops are sometimes given even when a nation turns from God. We've often observed that just as unbelievers are blessed along with believers, so the believers are often victims of disasters along with unbelievers: "[God] gives his sunlight to both the evil and the good, and he sends rain on the just and the unjust alike" (Matthew 5:45). Disasters come blindly and strike down people without regard to position, status, age, or morality. And natural disasters also do not discriminate according to people's religion. After the tsunami in Southeast Asia, reports began to filter in from the different religious groups, each claiming that God was on their side because they were miraculously spared.

For example, ten days after that tsunami, the *Chicago Tribune* reported that "a Sri Lankan priest's decision to leave a small coastal chapel unused on December 26 was a lifesaver." For no particular reason, the priest moved the mass from the beachside chapel to a church a mile from the coast. As a result, the service started forty-five minutes late, and when it was over, the tsunami struck. Even if the service had started on time, many of the parishioners would likely have already returned to their homes and been caught in the deadly waves. But because the mass was performed later than scheduled, the fifteen hundred people who stayed to the end of the service survived.[1]

The priest himself did not say this proved the truthfulness of the Catholic faith, but some of the parishioners believed the reason they were spared was because St. Joseph, the church in which the services were held, had a statue of the holy family. The coastal church that was totally destroyed did not.

I also heard a story of protection from Protestant evangelicals. In the town of Meulaboh, Indonesia, there are about four hundred Christians. They wanted to celebrate Christmas on December 25, but the Muslims, who made up the majority of the population, prohibited it. The Christians were told that if they wanted to honor the birth of Christ, they needed to go outside the city. So that's what they did, celebrating Christmas the next night on a hill. In the morning, the tsunami killed 80 percent of the people of the village, but all the Christians were spared.

But then in another area where the tsunami hit, Poorima Jayaratne had a different interpretation. Four houses next to hers were flattened, while three rooms in her house remained intact. Her survival was explained this way: "'Most of the people who lost relatives were Muslim,' [she] said . . . adding for good measure that two Christians were also missing."

She believed that Buddha protected her, and she pointed to a picture of him that hung on one of the remaining intact walls of her house, undisturbed by the massive destruction. Evidently, that was all she needed to confirm her faith.[2]

Muslims, however, also claimed victories because in one area along the coast, every building was leveled as far as the eye could see—except a white mosque. Did this show the superiority of the Muslim faith? Some people thought so.

Tragedies do indeed separate people into two camps, but those two groups are simply the living and the dead.

My point is clear: We should not seek confirmation of any particular religion in the disasters that pound our planet. Tragedies do indeed separate people into two camps, but those two groups are simply the living and the dead. Tragedies do not differentiate between good and evil people, nor between the right and the wrong religions.

In fact, sometimes the lines are blurred, as occurred in the recent series of tornadoes that blew through the southern United States. Fox News reported, "Macolee Muhammed accepted the prayer of a relief worker who stopped by what was left of her Birmingham home. It didn't matter that she was Muslim and he was a Southern Baptist. 'If you came here to help, the only person who sent you was God,' she said."[3]

With all of that said, however, I also believe that natural disasters are indeed God's megaphone. He is speaking to us even if He is not saying what some people claim to be hearing. Surely disasters teach us lessons, and as we shall see in the next chapter, they can also be previews of events to come.

Lessons We Can Learn

Even if God's ultimate purpose behind a disaster remains a mystery, we are given some clues as to what these tragedies should mean for us. It would be a mistake for us to allow disasters to come and go without seeing in them—through simple observation and the teaching of Jesus—certain lessons we should take to heart.

I visited the Pompeii exhibit when it was at the Field Museum in Chicago in 2005. I was fascinated by what the victims chose to take with them as they fled from their homes trying to escape the deadly eruption of Mount Vesuvius in AD 79. The volcanic eruption buried the city of Pompeii, Italy, in fifteen feet of pumice and ash, killing everyone. It seemed that people died trying to hoard the few treasures they could carry with them—necklaces, mirrors, and silver or gold coins. One display read, "Holding her family's wealth, the woman of the house died alongside her slaves." This woman tried to escape with her treasures but died with those who owned nothing. Natural disasters have a leveling effect on humanity; at the moment of death, we are all reduced to the same helplessness.

We Learn What Is Truly Valuable

Disasters help us to see what is truly valuable and what is not: tragedy separates the trivial from the important, the temporary from the eternal. When that tower in Siloam fell, no one mourned the loss of the bricks, but eighteen families mourned the loss of a husband, father, or brother.

In the wake of Hurricane Katrina, author Max Lucado said, "No one laments a lost plasma television or submerged SUV. No one runs through the streets yelling, 'My cordless drill is missing' or 'My golf clubs have washed away.' If they mourn, it is for people lost. If they rejoice, it is for people found."[4] He went on to say that raging hurricanes and broken levees have a way of prying our fingers off the things we love. As a survivor of the recent tornado in Alabama noted, "It makes you stop and think . . . we're here one minute and . . . gone the next."[5]

We are reminded of the words of Jesus: "Beware! Guard against every kind of greed. Life is not measured by how much you own" (Luke 12:15). As a pastor, I've seen how the suffering of a child or the death of a loved one suddenly gives people a whole new pair of glasses through which to view the world. True loss reveals if we have been giving most of our attention to things that don't really matter. Tragedy jerks us into reality and makes us realize that people matter more than things. Tragedy separates time on earth from eternity, this world from the next. And to further clarify our values, Jesus also said, "What do you benefit if you gain the whole world but lose your own soul? Is anything worth more than your soul?" (Matthew 16:26).

Disasters help us to see what is truly valuable and what is not: tragedy separates the trivial from the important, the temporary from the eternal.

I agree with John Piper, who said that natural disasters give Christians the opportunity to prove that no earthly treasure can compare with the value of knowing Christ. It's a reminder of Paul's words:

But whatever were gains to me I now consider loss
for the sake of Christ. What is more, I consider
everything a loss because of the surpassing worth
of knowing Christ Jesus my Lord, for whose sake
I have lost all things. I consider them garbage, that
I may gain Christ and be found in him, not having
a righteousness of my own that comes from the law,
but that which is through faith in Christ.

PHILIPPIANS 3:7-9, NIV

Those who know Jesus have a treasure that suffering and
death can never take from them.

We Learn about the Mixture of Evil and Good in Us All

I've always been fascinated by human nature. I marvel at both
human goodness and human evil and how the two can sometimes exist side by side when tragedy strikes. After Hurricane
Katrina, we saw many stories of heroic and sacrificial rescues
in New Orleans, many people risking their own lives for the
sake of others. In the recent disaster in Japan, heroes were
going into the crippled nuclear power plants, knowing the
probability of radiation exposure, to try to stop the problem
from getting worse.

Yet at the same time, we also saw raw human nature in
all of its horridness. Looters in New Orleans grabbed what
they could for their families from stores abandoned during the disaster. But far worse than that were the rumors
of rape, beatings, and murders that supposedly took place
in the Superdome—the place where tens of thousands were

trying to find shelter and safety. Some people deliberately set fires; sometimes people shot at rescue helicopters. Those who returned to clean up after the disaster were surprised by the amount of pornography floating about after the waters passed through homes and flooded the streets.

Volunteers also arrived in force after the Southeast Asia tsunami, many making great personal sacrifices to help the victims. But at the same time, we also heard about the horrid sex trade in countries such as Thailand and Sri Lanka. Reports filtered through about young children being kidnapped and exploited by sexual perverts who surfaced to take advantage of these precious little ones. As if being orphaned was not enough, those children became prey for the most despicable acts of human cruelty imaginable.

As I discussed in chapter 1, the world of physical nature is a reflection of the moral world of human beings. Just as undersea earthquakes let loose massive tsunamis that engulfed Southeast Asia and Japan, and just as the breached levees in New Orleans released a flood of water over much of the city, so the evil of the human heart was also set free to do its damage in the midst of these disasters. If it weren't for legal and social restraints that keep human nature in check, this world would be overwhelmed by an unstoppable tsunami of evil.

However—and this is important—we must realize that there is a mixture of evil and goodness in all of us. Aleksandr Solzhenitsyn, the 1970 Nobel Prize winner for literature, said in *The Gulag Archipelago*, "If only it were all so simple! If only there were evil people somewhere insidiously committing evil deeds, and it were necessary only to separate them from the rest of us and destroy them. But the line dividing good and evil cuts through the heart of every human being."[6] There's no such thing as a "sin-free zone" for good people because the line between good and evil does not run through the human race, but through every human heart!

There's no such thing as a "sin-free zone" for good people because the line between good and evil runs through every human heart!

We all need redemption. Left to ourselves, we are filled with suspicion, greed, and fear. We will take advantage of others to enrich ourselves; we will become obsessed with what we can get for ourselves, caring little for the welfare of our neighbors. Tragedy brings the good, the bad, and the ugly to the surface, and human nature is exposed for all to see.

We Learn about the Uncertainty of Life

Natural disasters confirm the words of the biblical writer James: "How do you know what your life will be like tomorrow? Your life is like the morning fog—it's here a little while, then it's gone" (James 4:14). People who lost their lives in a natural disaster did not wake up that morning thinking to themselves, *This could be my last day on earth.* Unfortunately, few of us believe that what happened to them could happen to us. But the tower of Siloam, like any natural disaster, fell unexpectedly, without prior warning.

When you read the obituaries of people who have died in sudden calamities, do you visualize your own name there? We all know someone who died unexpectedly—a car accident, a heart attack. When we grieve with the families, we should remind ourselves that we, too, could die at any moment. In the same way, natural disasters remind us that death might be just around the next corner.

I read about one couple who left California for fear of earthquakes and died in a tornado in Missouri. Each of us will die at the time God has appointed for us—no matter where we are or what we're doing. Our lives are simply on loan from God. He gives life, and He takes it away—and He can take it whenever and however He chooses. Death is determined for all of us, whether by cancer, an accident, or a natural disaster. The Bible teaches that death is a scheduled, divine appointment.

Disasters, in the words of apologist Dave Miller, remind us that "human existence on Earth was not intended to be permanent. Rather, the Creator intended life on Earth to serve as a temporary interval of time . . . in which people are given the opportunity to attend to their spiritual condition as it relates to God's will for living. Natural disasters provide people with conclusive evidence that life on Earth is brief and uncertain."[7]

We Learn the Danger of Thinking We Are in Control

Tragedies rid us of the overconfidence we have that we are in control of our destinies.

Often in tragedies we hear stories of people who thought they could defy the odds, who thought they could control their destinies. We always hear about people who stay their ground as hurricanes descend upon an area—they're boarding up windows and buying bottled water believing they can wait it out. Bravery? No. Unwise? Certainly.

I heard the story of Edgar Hollingsworth who refused to leave his home in New Orleans when Hurricane Katrina was approaching. His wife, Lillian, kissed him good-bye, and although she and his grandchildren begged him to leave, he refused. "Don't worry about me," he said. "When I was in the army, I went a whole month without eating." He believed the storm would not hit his neighborhood but go around instead, the same way all the previous ones had.

Edgar's relatives thought of forcing him into a car, but they did not want to make him angry. "All of a sudden he got real stubborn," Lillian said. The next day the storm came and the waters rose. They tried to make contact with Edgar, but the phone lines were down and they knew they had to leave the city. Lillian prayed that someone would rescue her husband, and on some days, she felt confident that he would be fine.

Meanwhile, rescue teams had put an X and a zero on the house in which Edgar was living, indicating that they had checked the house and were confident no one was inside. But when another rescue team went to search for abandoned animals, they discovered Edgar, almost skeletal, on an upended couch. They were shocked when Edgar, whom they thought was dead, suddenly gasped for air. Emergency crews hurried to his house and immediately began lifesaving measures.

The next day, Lillian stared in shock at the picture of her husband on the front page of a Baton Rouge newspaper. She found out where he had been taken and rushed to his side, but despite heroic efforts, Edgar died twenty minutes after she arrived. Clearly, Edgar was not in charge of his own destiny—and neither was anyone else.[8]

We Learn the Need to Take God Seriously

Unexpected tragedy ends the illusion that our lives are predictable and our futures certain. Many of us meander through our days believing that the good life consists of money, pleasure, and leisure and that the not-so-good life is one of poverty, struggle, and servitude. But Jesus told a story that proved how such superficial evaluations can be deceptive. According to the story, a rich man who enjoyed life found himself in torment after he died, whereas a beggar who suffered on earth found himself in bliss (Luke 16:19-31). This sudden reversal of fortune reminds us that our judgments of today might have to be severely revised tomorrow! In times of disaster, when we are faced with the reality of death, we are also forced to take God seriously.

In times of disaster, when we are faced with the reality of death, we are also forced to take God seriously.

In *The Screwtape Letters*, C. S. Lewis imagines a lead demon, Screwtape, giving advice to Wormwood, a demonic underling, for how to deceive humans. The younger demon is all for starting a war, but Screwtape knows better. Yes, in a time of war there is a lot of cruelty, which the demons of course enjoy, but people tend to turn to the Enemy (Screwtape's reference to God) in times of such huge crisis and possible impending death. Screwtape suggests instead that Wormwood focus on making people think they have all the time in the world to continue to live in whatever way they please. Lewis believes—and I agree—that "contented worldliness" is one of the devil's best weapons during times of peace. But when disasters come, this weapon of thinking we have lots of time becomes worthless. Suddenly the reality of the frailty and uncertainty of life hits us full force—and we start asking questions about our own eternal future.

This is one reason we will never know all of God's purposes in natural disasters. We simply do not know the countless number of spiritually "content" people who are forced to take God seriously in a time of crisis. Many survivors choose to harden their hearts against God; others turn to Him in repentance and faith. And even to those of us who watch these calamities at a safe distance, God is saying, "Prepare for your own death . . . it may be soon!"

But now we must turn our attention to a more difficult topic: Are natural disasters specific judgments of God? How should we interpret them from a divine perspective? In the midst of judgment, does God remember mercy?

Keep reading.

QUESTIONS FOR DISCUSSION

1. God dealt with His people differently in the Old Testament than He does today. Why do you think this is so?

2. What specific lessons has God taught you during the "storms" in your own life?

3. Why do you think God sometimes chooses to treat good people and evil people the same in this life?

4. What changes would you make in your own life if you knew you were going to die in a natural disaster within a month?

ARE DISASTERS THE JUDGMENTS OF GOD?

Nation will go to war against nation, and kingdom against kingdom.
There will be famines and earthquakes in many parts of the world.
But all this is only the first of the birth pains, with more to come.

MATTHEW 24:7-8

WE HAVE LEARNED that we can make the case that yes, indeed, God is involved in natural disasters—He allows them to occur, and they can act as His megaphone to teach us some important lessons.

But we still have another question: are disasters the judgments of God? That is, do these things happen because God is judging sin in our world?

Again, the answer isn't easy, but let's look at this logically.

Natural Disasters as Judgments

Let's return first to the words of Jesus when He spoke about the collapsed tower of Siloam: "You will perish, too, unless you repent of your sins and turn to God" (Luke 13:3). Jesus used the example of those who died unexpectedly when the tower of Siloam fell on them to make the point that death can come at any time and we must repent *now* if we do not want to perish. The same is true for everyone today: death can still come unexpectedly—natural disasters being one of those ways where death can occur suddenly and with little warning. Therefore, since death can come at any moment, we would be wise to repent, turn to God, and be saved. Then when we die, we will not perish for eternity but be resurrected to eternal life. For those who repent and believe, death will still occur—and may indeed occur in a natural disaster—but it is a gateway into eternal life. For the unrepentant person, however, death will still occur—and may indeed occur in a natural disaster—but that person will face sudden judgment without warning, a judgment more terrifying than a natural disaster could ever be.

Follow this thought carefully: the fact that natural disasters happen randomly without regard to race, age, religion, or lifestyle does not mean that they cannot be considered as present judgments and a preview of coming punishment on the entire world for sin. We've all had to sit through previews in a theater while waiting for the real movie to begin. Natural disasters are a preview, a heads-up warning that more severe judgment is ahead.

I disagree with columnist and senior editor Dennis Behreandt, who wrote in *The New American* that natural disasters cannot be judgments because they happen indiscriminately. He writes, "There are plenty of people who have turned away from God and lead lives of sin and depravity, harming others and violating their rights. Why not just punish the murderers, the rapists, and the thieves? Surely God can differentiate between those who try to live godly lives and those who spurn both God and man alike."[1]

Of course, if God wished, He could send natural disasters only to the wicked, but He doesn't do it that way. As I have shown, godly people can and do experience punishments on this earth, along with all other kinds of pain and suffering, just as ungodly people do. We also know that upheavals of nature happen in specific geographical areas regardless of the relative godliness or ungodliness of the people who live there—earthquakes occur along fault lines, hurricanes and tsunamis hit coastlines. But just because they have "natural" reasons for occurring and just because they only happen in certain areas does not mean that disasters can't be considered judgments from God. *Natural disasters are indeed judgments, for the same reason that death and destruction are judgments of God on all people because of sin.*

Even though Christ died for our sins, we as Christians will still die because of sin. Remember that death *is* a judgment for sin. "For the wages of sin is death, but the free gift of God is eternal life through Christ Jesus our Lord" (Romans 6:23). Jesus removed the sting of death, but it will come to us nonetheless. Think of it this way: the whole earth is under a curse, and we as believers are a part of that corruption. Clearly, even those who are godly also become victims of tragedy and judgment in this fallen world. The Curse will not be fully lifted until we are fully redeemed. And as to Behreandt's comment above, God will indeed one day differentiate between those who live godly lives and those who don't—He just is not doing it yet.

In natural disasters, God intensifies the Curse that is already upon nature and, for that matter, upon us. When

In natural disasters, God intensifies the Curse that is already upon nature and, for that matter, upon us.

we look at it this way, we realize that natural disasters happen every day as thousands of people die from disease, accidents, and tragedies of various kinds. Natural disasters only catch our attention when they are of such a great magnitude that they capture headlines, citing many simultaneous deaths and unbelievable devastation to property. These disasters are really only a dramatic acceleration of what is happening all the time.

Is God Angry?

So is God angry with the people of any location where disasters happen? Was He angry with the people in Missouri or the southern part of the United States, or Japan, or Sri Lanka, or even Portugal many centuries ago? Is that why He sent disasters to those locations? Here in America, I often hear statements such as, "If we don't repent, God is going to judge America!" We forget that America is already under judgment—continuous, *present* judgment—as is every person in every country on the entire planet. In Deuteronomy, God warned the Jews that if they did not repent, they would experience a series of judgments, culminating in the destruction of their families. "You will watch as your sons and daughters are taken away as slaves. Your heart will break for them, but you won't be able to help them" (Deuteronomy 28:32). Indeed, children and their parents would be starving, and there would be no way to save them (Deuteronomy 28:54-57).

The destruction of the family is certainly one of God's judgments against America, a nation that has indeed turned away from God. The spread of immorality, pornography, and even same-sex marriage is proof that God's hand is being removed from us as we plunge headlong into personal and national rebellion. As a result, our children are suffering from predators, from sexual abuse within their own families, and from self-absorbed, uncaring parents. All sin has immediate consequences, but when it accumulates, there are future judgments of various kinds. Natural disasters are just one more way that God reveals Himself and begs us to turn from our wicked ways and prepare for a better world.

So we are correct in saying natural disasters are judgments, but mistaken when we go beyond this and say that these judgments target only one religion, one race, or even one particular kind of sinner. Yes, it may be true that the countries hit by tsunamis, such as Thailand and Sri Lanka, were judged because of their exploitation of children. But then we have to ask why was Bangkok, the hub of the sex-trade industry, spared? Was New Orleans a more sinful city than Las Vegas? New Orleans was destroyed, but Las Vegas, the capital of gambling and prostitution and all other kinds of sins, still stands in all its bright-lights glory. And why did God allow the earthquake and resultant tsunami to hit the northern part of Japan and not the densely populated city of Tokyo? Was the fact that the nuclear reactors were damaged some kind of divine judgment on nuclear power? Or were those people in the little town of Sendai more wicked than those in Tokyo? Do you see where we get into trouble trying to read God's mind when it comes to why disasters happen?

Natural disasters are just one more way that God reveals Himself and begs us to turn from our wicked ways and prepare for a better world.

Only God knows for sure if particular disasters target particular judgments for specific sins.

As we see all the time in this life, judgments by way of natural disasters appear to be haphazard. Sometimes, contrary to what we would expect, the wicked are spared the catastrophes that kill the righteous. However, God has different purposes in such disasters.

First, His purpose for *those who die* is to be brought into His presence where each will be judged individually, fairly, and eternally. Some will be invited into His presence and others will be banished. "They will go away into eternal punishment, but the righteous will go into eternal life" (Matthew 25:46).

Second, His purposes for *the survivors* are to warn them of the uncertainty of life and the urgency to prepare for death. Volunteers are given the opportunity to show their love and care for those who suffer. For some, calamities are punishment; for others, they are given new life through repentance and renewed devotion to God. What to us appears random no doubt has specific purposes known only to the Almighty.

So we return to the question: is God mad? His justifiable anger is directed at all who refuse to acknowledge His Word: "God shows his anger from heaven against all sinful, wicked people who suppress the truth by their wickedness" (Romans 1:18). Yet He is gracious to those who respond to His mercy as found in Jesus Christ. "Since we have been made right in God's sight by the blood of Christ, he will certainly save us from God's condemnation" (Romans 5:9).

Eventually God's focus comes down to the individual. Those who come under the protection of Christ's grace are especially loved and accepted, and those who spurn His mercy are targeted for judgment, either now or later. The good news, of course, is that everyone who is reading this book has a wonderful opportunity to take advantage of God's undeserved grace. "God saved you by his grace when you believed. And you can't take credit for this; it is a gift from God" (Ephesians 2:8).

When God sees any nation, He sees those who are under His wrath as well as those who are objects of His special grace. Yes, there are times when an entire nation seems to turn from God and the nation is judged. But there also is a remnant of true believers whose lives please our Father in heaven. We will have to wait for eternity for the outcome of all of God's purposes to be revealed.

Disasters and the End Times

Nature reflects God's gracious attributes, but also His attributes of anger and justice. In the book of Job, a discerning young theologian, Elihu, says of God:

> He directs the snow to fall on the earth and tells the
> rain to pour down. . . . God's breath sends the ice,

freezing wide expanses of water. He loads the clouds
with moisture, and they flash with his lightning.
The clouds churn about at his direction. They do
whatever he commands throughout the earth. He
makes these things happen either to punish people
or to show his unfailing love.

JOB 37:6, 10-13

*He makes these things happen either to punish people or to
show his unfailing love.* We like to think that God is only in
control of the positive side of nature: the sunshine, the irre-
sistible lure of calm waters, and the starry heavens. But, as
we have learned, God is in charge of the totality of nature.
If the goodness of God is seen in the blessings of nature, His
judgments are seen in the "cursing" of nature. Either way,
nature instructs us, helping us
understand God better.

*The starry heavens reflect the
glory of God; calm winds and
sunshine remind us of the mercy
of God; the upheavals of nature
demonstrate the judgment of God.*

The starry heavens reflect
the glory of God; calm winds
and sunshine remind us of the
mercy of God; the upheavals of
nature demonstrate the judg-
ment of God. If the sunshine is a taste of the beauty of heaven,
the hurricane is a taste of the suffering of hell. "Notice how
God is both kind and severe. He is severe toward those who
disobeyed, but kind to you if you continue to trust in his
kindness" (Romans 11:22). We should not be surprised that
nature is both kind and severe.

Jesus confirmed that end-times calamities were a sign of

the end of the age. "There will be famines and earthquakes in many parts of the world. But all this is only the first of the birth pains" (Matthew 24:7-8). Interestingly, the number of earthquakes on the earth has increased over the centuries, and their number is increasing every year. Only the powerful ones make headlines.

Depending on how you classify them, at least three—and maybe even four—natural disasters will accompany Jesus' return to earth:

> For as the lightning flashes in the east and shines to
> the west, so it will be when the Son of Man comes.
> Just as the gathering of vultures shows there is a
> carcass nearby, so these signs indicate that the end
> is near. Immediately after the anguish of those days,
> the sun will be darkened, the moon will give no
> light, the stars will fall from the sky, and the powers
> in the heavens will be shaken. And then at last, the
> sign that the Son of Man is coming will appear in
> the heavens, and there will be deep mourning among
> all the peoples of the earth.
>
> MATTHEW 24:27-30

However, even as we read these words, we must not be too hasty in thinking that we know when and how the end will come. In 2005, a *New York Times* article titled "Doomsday: The Latest Word If Not the Last," gave some examples of how quickly Christians rush to conclusions about the end of the world.[2] We heard it when Israeli troops captured the Old

City of Jerusalem in 1967, and later in 1994 when Yitzhak Rabin, prime minister of Israel in the late 1970s, worked out a peace accord with the Palestinian leader Yasser Arafat. And now we hear again that the end of the world is near because of the growing number of natural disasters. I have in my library a book, *The Last Days Are Here Again.* As you are no doubt aware, life on this planet has not yet ceased to exist, even though so many have predicted its demise.

Yet it is important to realize that convulsions of nature will indeed eventually be a part of God's sovereign judgment. Consider this future "natural disaster," which appears to be the real movie that follows the preview:

> I watched as the Lamb broke the sixth seal, and there was a great earthquake. The sun became as dark as black cloth, and the moon became as red as blood. Then the stars of the sky fell to the earth like green figs falling from a tree shaken by a strong wind. The sky was rolled up like a scroll, and all of the mountains and islands were moved from their places.
>
> Then everyone—the kings of the earth, the rulers, the generals, the wealthy, the powerful, and every slave and free person—all hid themselves in the caves and among the rocks of the mountains. And they cried to the mountains and the rocks, "Fall on us and hide us from the face of the one who sits on the throne and from the wrath of the Lamb. For the great day of their wrath has come, and who is able to survive?"
>
> REVELATION 6:12-17

Some liberal theologians would have us believe that judgment is not coming. Their theology teaches that God seeks the happiness of His creation above all else; therefore, God would never judge us for our sins or commit anyone to hell. They claim that love wins and this love cancels all serious judgment. That kind of God may be convenient and easy to believe in, but that is not the God of the Bible. This "domesticated God" is contradicted by the natural disasters in the world. Those who believe in such a God cannot make any sense of disasters, and it appears that their God does not have the power then to keep His people safe and happy. They cannot conceive of disasters as judgment because they don't believe in judgment. They are left with questions and no hope of logical answers.

But this is not our God. The true God of the Bible does not delight in human suffering, but He does delight in the triumph of truth and justice and the completion of His hidden purposes—and those things sometimes must happen by way of natural disasters. That's how it is now, and that's how it will be at the end of time.

> *The true God of the Bible does not delight in human suffering, but He does delight in the triumph of truth and justice and the completion of His hidden purposes.*

The Escape Route

The good news is this: we escape coming judgment by repentance. "You will perish . . . unless you repent of your sins and turn to God" (Luke 13:3). Yes, it would be wonderful if the citizens of any city and nation where disasters occur would do just that—repent of their sins and turn to God. But we know that as believers, we must lead the way. Peter wrote, "For the time has come for judgment, and it must begin with God's household. And if judgment begins with us, what terrible fate awaits those who have never obeyed God's Good News? And also, 'If the righteous are barely saved, what will happen to godless sinners?'" (1 Peter 4:17-18). God is shouting, but is anyone listening?

Remember, too, that mercy is included in every act of judgment that occurs in natural disasters. We should take a page from believers in Scotland who, following a 1741 hurricane, organized prayer societies. What began in one church spread to other churches, and soon the churches were filled with people praying and asking God to help them in their time of need. "People were pleading with God to multiply the work begun among them."[3]

Cleansed people ought to be renewed people. What will it take for us to learn the lessons from these disasters and take those lessons into our world?

Saved or Lost?

As already noted, natural disasters don't divide people into economic or age or moral categories, but they *do* ultimately divide the human race into two categories—the living and the dead. The dead have no opportunity to repent, no second chance at life and redemption. For the living, the opportunity of repentance is still at hand. "Just as each person is destined to die once and after that comes judgment, so also

Christ died once for all time as a sacrifice to take away the sins of many people. He will come again, not to deal with our sins, but to bring salvation to all who are eagerly waiting for him" (Hebrews 9:27-28).

In April 1912, when the great ocean liner *Titanic* sank in the North Atlantic, 1,517 people knowingly went to a watery grave. Even if we attribute the sinking of that ship to a series of human errors, God most assuredly could have kept it from sinking. This is another reminder that the God who permits such unthinkable tragedies is one to be feared.

After the news of *Titanic*'s tragedy reached the world, the challenge was how to inform the passengers' relatives whether their loved ones had survived. At the White Star Line's office in Liverpool, England, a huge board was set up. On one side was a cardboard sign with the heading KNOWN TO BE SAVED, and on the other, a cardboard sign with the words KNOWN TO BE LOST. Hundreds of people gathered to intently watch the updates, holding their breaths when a messenger brought new information to be posted.

Although the travelers on the *Titanic* were either first-, second-, or third-class passengers, after the ship went down, there were only two categories: the living and the dead. Likewise, on the Day of Judgment, there will be only two classes: the saved and the lost—those who repented and turned to God for salvation and those who did not. There are only two eternal destinations—heaven or hell.

God shouts from heaven, "You will perish, too, unless you repent of your sins and turn to God" (Luke 13:3).

QUESTIONS FOR DISCUSSION

1. Discuss the statement, "Natural disasters are judgments of God." Discuss common misunderstandings of this phrase and brainstorm how you might clear up those misunderstandings.

2. How would you answer the question, "Is God mad at us?"

3. What is the role of a Christian in the wake of a natural disaster?

4. In what ways do you see natural disasters as a preview of the future?

5. What would a nation look like if all of its people repented of their sins?

CAN WE STILL TRUST GOD?

God might kill me, but I have no other hope.

JOB 13:15

AS WE HAVE SEEN, natural disasters occur constantly on this planet. Can we trust a sovereign God who could at any moment put an end to such suffering—but doesn't? A God who could have prevented the catastrophes that have pounded the world throughout the centuries? A God who could have made sure that children weren't hurt or orphaned or kidnapped into the sex trade as a result of a natural disaster?

An intellectual answer—even a true one—never satisfies the human heart. Being told of God's eternal and transcendent purposes in the wake of a disaster doesn't help much if you're suffering or if you've lost someone you love. Information itself cannot heal a broken heart; only God's grace can do that.

Yet even as we begin to comprehend that we will never understand God (nor should we—if we could, then we probably wouldn't need Him), that doesn't mean we have to endure things unquestioningly. God encourages us to ask Him questions and seek His answers. "Keep on asking, and you will receive what you ask for. Keep on seeking, and you will find. Keep on knocking, and the door will be opened to you" (Matthew 7:7). The pages of the Bible are filled with people who asked God tough questions. Sometimes God answered; sometimes He didn't. But in all cases, the questioner came away with a sense of God's awesome greatness. His plans stretch from eternity past into eternity future, far beyond what our little minds can take in.

People in the Bible asked God tough questions. Sometimes God answered; sometimes He didn't. But in all cases, the questioner came away with a sense of God's awesome greatness.

Ecclesiastes tells us that God has "planted eternity in the human heart" (Ecclesiastes 3:11). In other words, we as human beings have a God-given awareness of the infinite, of something outside of ourselves and outside of time itself—enough for us to be in awe of our God, who is infinite.

But is it enough for us to trust Him?

Beyond Our Understanding

We know that God is all-powerful and has all knowledge, but when we look at our world and see the horrors that unfold every day, we wonder if He is also good. Does He deserve our trust? If we answer yes—and I hope we do—we must agree that our good God has a good reason for allowing (or ordaining) disasters. If we answer no, if we do not trust God and we believe that He did not already have a plan and a higher purpose in these evils, then they would be happening outside of His control. He would have to run around trying to clean up in order to make the best of tragic events, somehow hoping that they might actually come together into some big cosmic plan in the end.

Thankfully, God is not confused. Our good God does indeed have a good plan that encompasses every event that has occurred and will occur. Every disaster is in the grand scope of His cosmic plan. It may not help us to understand or to feel better when we ourselves face devastation, but we can at least trust in the fact that the world has not spun out of control. A plan is still in place. A good plan.

This is an important message. I believe we *should* speak about God's power and control, and we should also console ourselves with the certainty of an afterlife. As I noted earlier in the book, we should be wary about glib answers that would seem to make light of people's very real suffering. I also believe that we should not have our faith upset by every random, accidental death. I must emphasize the point I discussed earlier: if natural disasters are out of God's control, then my life and my future are also out of God's control. But if I believe that my life and future are in God's control, then I must also believe that the natural disasters are in His control as well.

At this point, we should return to the question raised in the first chapter: is this the best of all possible worlds? If we saw everything from God's viewpoint—if we could see the ultimate end of God's purposes and His own glory—we would have to agree that His plan is right and good. This is not the best of all possible worlds, but from the standpoint of eternity, the best of all architects chose the best of all possible blueprints. This does not mean that God is pleased with evil, but it does mean that He is pleased with how He will use it toward wise and good ends.

What would you do if you had God's power for twenty-four hours? Of course, we all answer that we would rid the world of poverty, wars, and disasters. We would put an end to all forms of evil and create a paradise for everyone. *If only!*

What would you do if you had God's power for twenty-four hours?

On the other hand, if we were also given God's wisdom, I'm convinced that we would leave things as they are! For our all-wise and all-powerful heavenly Father has a hidden agenda that makes sense out of it all. There is meaning in the madness.[1]

However—and this is important—if we wonder what God's ultimate, hidden purpose is in natural disasters, we can only say that He is relentless in the pursuit of His own glory. The following verses help make that clear:

> Pick up your staff and raise your hand over the sea.
> Divide the water so the Israelites can walk through
> the middle of the sea on dry ground. And I will
> harden the hearts of the Egyptians, and they will
> charge in after the Israelites. My great glory will
> be displayed through Pharaoh and his troops, his
> chariots, and his charioteers. When my glory is

displayed through them, all Egypt will see my glory
and know that I am the LORD!

EXODUS 14:16-18

I will gather all nations and peoples together, and
they will see my glory. I will perform a sign among
them. And I will send those who survive to be
messengers to the nations—to Tarshish, to the
Libyans and Lydians (who are famous as archers),
to Tubal and Greece, and to all the lands beyond the
sea that have not heard of my fame or seen my glory.
There they will declare my glory to the nations.

ISAIAH 66:18-19

Give the people of Sidon this message from the
Sovereign LORD: "I am your enemy, O Sidon, and I
will reveal my glory by what I do to you. When I bring
judgment against you and reveal my holiness among
you, everyone watching will know that I am the LORD."

EZEKIEL 28:22

When he comes on that day, he will receive glory
from his holy people—praise from all who believe.

2 THESSALONIANS 1:10

You are worthy, O Lord our God, to receive glory
and honor and power. For you created all things,
and they exist because you created what you pleased.

REVELATION 4:11

God is allowed—because He is God. We've already acknowledged that God does give us some insight into His divine mind, but let us humbly confess that we see only glimpses of the eternal purpose.

After years of studying the problem of reconciling the suffering of this world with God's mercy, I have concluded that there is no solution that will completely satisfy our minds, much less the mind of a skeptic. "God is greater than we can understand" (Job 36:26). He has simply chosen not to reveal all the pieces of the puzzle. *God is more mysterious than we care to admit.*

It sounds like a cop-out, doesn't it? But it really isn't. A God whom we could completely understand would not be God at all. He would be like us—and we are fallible, sinful, and can only see what is directly in front of us. That's not someone you would want to trust your life—and eternity—to.

After all the theological essays have been written and all of the debaters have become silent, we have to admit that there is much we still don't understand. We can only stand in awe of this great mystery. Theology professor John Stackhouse has written:

> The God of predestination, the God of worldwide
> providence, the God who created all and sustains
> all and thus ultimately is responsible for all—
> this God has revealed to us only glimpses of the
> divine cosmic plan. God has not let us see in any
> comprehensive way the sense in suffering, the

method in the madness. God has chosen, instead, to remain hidden in mystery.[2]

Yes, God has chosen to remain a mystery. In his book *On First Principles*, first-century theologian Origen described what Paul meant in Romans 11:33 when he wrote that God's judgments are "unsearchable" (NIV) and His ways "unfathomable" (NASB). Just read these words:

> Paul did not say that God's judgments were hard to search out but that they could not be searched out at all. He did not say that God's ways were hard to find out but that they were impossible to find out. For however far one may advance in the search and make progress through an increasing earnest study, even when aided and enlightened in the mind by God's grace, he will never be able to reach the final goal of his inquiries.[3]

Sure, we've been promised to "ask and receive," but I believe that even if God *did* answer some of our queries when we demand answers, we would walk away scratching our heads. We simply would not understand. It would be beyond our ability to understand.

However, I believe strongly that it is not necessary for us to understand the hidden purposes of the Almighty in order to believe that such purposes exist. I also believe that someday we will be granted the ability to understand. "For now we see in a mirror dimly, but then face to face; now I know in part, but then I will know fully just as I also have been fully known" (1 Corinthians 13:12, NASB). We see all of the jumbled threads on the back side of the tapestry right now; only God sees the beautiful and intricate pattern from the front.

The New Testament realistically shows the pain and evil of this world, but assures us that the future will make sense of the past. "What we suffer now is nothing compared to the glory he will reveal to us later" (Romans 8:18). In the future, the unseen will give meaning to that which is seen. Eternity will interpret what happened in time. Meanwhile, we live by promises, not explanations.

In the future, the unseen will give meaning to that which is seen. Eternity will interpret what happened in time. Meanwhile, we live by promises, not explanations.

At a Loss without God

Sometimes people will not be satisfied with your explanation that God is beyond our understanding. They see that as a nonanswer. Indeed, many people have chosen instead to believe that God simply does not exist. These people are called atheists (or naturalists).

What often happens, however, is that these people who claim that God does not exist get all heated and argumentative when tragedy strikes. I've often heard the argument that if a God who is omnipotent (all-powerful), omniscient (all-knowing), and loving existed, He would do away with evil and suffering. Since horrendous suffering exists, the atheist says, God must either be weak, unknowing, or sadistic. And who wants to believe in that kind of a God? Much better to believe that there is no God at all. Atheists therefore look about, see the misery millions endure, and ask sarcastically, "Where was God when the tsunami happened?" And they defy anyone to give an answer.

However, it's important to understand that this very question, coming from an atheist, is illegitimate and irrational. To ask the question, "Where was God?" is to assume the existence of God. An atheist, who claims that God does not exist, cannot even ask the question.

If there were not a creator God—if we are but a complicated combination of atoms that sprang into existence randomly—then the very idea of good and evil or better and best could not exist. After all, atheists believe that atoms have arranged themselves blindly according to haphazard patterns and whatever is, just *is*.

So if the atheist/naturalist asks where God was when a disaster occurred, then that person is assuming a moral framework that can only exist if God exists. Based on atheistic premises, there can be no spiritual substance such as soul or mind, only patterns of physical particles. Naturalists are in the unhappy position of having to maintain that matter can think, that matter can ask questions about which arrangement of matter is good and which is evil. Clearly, notions about good or evil cannot arise from atoms that existed in primordial slime.

Carefully considered, atheism is both contrary to logic and defies the deepest longings of the human soul. Remember Ecclesiastes? God "has planted eternity in the human heart" (Ecclesiastes 3:11). We long for something more—we instinctively know there is more than just this life on this planet. We were created for more, for *better*.

C. S. Lewis makes the same point when he argues that only God can account for the moral law—the understanding of right and wrong—that exists in all of us. During his days as an atheist, Lewis argued against God because the universe appeared so cruel and unjust. Then he realized that the very fact that he was thinking about "justice" and thus assuming that some things were "right" and others were "wrong" meant that there was a standard for these things—a standard that had to come from somewhere (and certainly did not originate with him). He went on to argue that the moral law—the understanding of right and wrong embedded within each of us—is a better reflection of God than the universe itself: "You find out more about God from the Moral Law than from the universe in general just as you find out more about a man by listening to his conversation than by looking at a house he has built."[4]

In an atheistic world, a world without God, evil can never be made to serve a higher purpose and suffering can never be redeemed. It just *is*. It has no meaning. Suicide would be attractive, for there would be no point in staying around trying to make this world a better place—because it simply can't happen.

A Jewish friend of mine, who is also an atheist, admitted that he felt some disquiet of spirit knowing that Hitler would never be judged for what he did. Because my friend is an atheist, he believes in no God and therefore no judgment or justice. He has no hope that there will be a final judgment to set the record straight. He ruefully admitted that without eternity, the events of time can never be redeemed or made right. It is indeed a sad way to live. Atheism satisfies neither the mind nor the heart; it isn't logical or helpful. And yet atheists persist in asking questions about good and evil for one reason: they may try to deny it, but they are created in the image of God. They have a soul, they have a basic understanding when something is right or wrong, and they have a longing for eternity that they have squelched because they cannot make sense of it. Ravi Zacharias says that such a person may claim that God is dead, "but the questions from his soul at a time like this reveal that he cannot kill Him completely."[5]

"O Katrina, have mercy on us!" a sign read in New Orleans before the hurricane hit. If we do not turn to the living God in a crisis, we will turn to the impersonal god of nature or we will manufacture some other deity in our own minds. Atheism simply cannot abide for long in the thoughtful human heart.

Keeping the Faith

So where does that leave us? As believers made in the image of God, as thoughtful people who understand right from wrong and see the disasters in our world as horribly wrong, where do we turn when God seems so distant, unfathomable, unsearchable? We're still asking the question, "Can we trust Him?" Martin Luther, in pondering the mystery of God's ways, urges us to "flee the hidden God and run to Christ." Now, of course, the "hidden God" and the God who was made flesh in Christ are one and the same; they are not separate divinities between whom we must choose.

But as Stackhouse (quoted earlier) points out, it is precisely because the two are one that Luther's advice works. He writes, "One must run away from the mysteries of God's providence about which we cannot know enough to understand (because God has revealed so little about them), and run toward Jesus Christ in whom we find God adequately revealed."[6] Jesus assures us in His Word that He is for us and that nothing will separate us from His love.

Look at the world and it might be hard to believe that God loves us and cares about us. At the very least, we could argue that God's attributes are ambiguous—at times it seems that He cares about us, and at other times He seems distant, indifferent, even callous. Nature has great beauty, but it also has great danger. If we just looked at nature, we would not know whether God intended to punish us at the end of life or forgive us.

If we want to discover whether God cares about His creation, we have to look beyond this world and beyond nature to His revelation of Himself in His Word and through His Son, the Living Word.

If we want to discover whether God cares about His creation, we have to look beyond this world and beyond nature to His revelation of Himself in His Word and through His Son, the Living Word. There we find hope that we could never discover on our own: "For God so loved the world, that he gave his only begotten Son, that whosoever believeth in him should not perish, but have everlasting life" (John 3:16, KJV).

In his book *The Silence of God*, Sir Robert Anderson wrestles with the apparent indifference of God to human pain and tragedy. After asking all the important *why* questions, he writes the following:

> But of all the questions which immediately concern
> us, there is not one which the Cross of Christ has
> left unanswered. Men point to the sad incidents
> of human life on earth, and they ask, "Where is
> the love of God?" God points to that Cross as the
> unreserved manifestation of love so inconceivably
> infinite as to answer every challenge and silence
> all doubt forever. And that Cross is not merely
> the public proof of what God has accomplished;
> it is the earnest of all that He has promised. The
> crowning mystery of God is Christ, for in Him "are
> all the treasures of wisdom and knowledge hidden."
> And those hidden treasures are yet to be unfolded.
> It is the Divine purpose to "gather together in one
> all things in Christ." *Sin has broken the harmony*
> *of creation, but that harmony shall yet be restored by*
> *the supremacy of our now despised and rejected Lord.*[7]
> (italics added)

Anderson goes on to explain that it was in the power of these truths that the martyrs died. Surely those who were set to be executed for their faith prayed for deliverance, but none came. Heaven was silent. Yet some reports say that when some Christian martyrs were marched to their death in France, they sang so loudly, the authorities hired a band to drown out the sound of their hymns! No sights were seen, no voices heard, no deliverance granted. They looked in vain for some external proof that God was with them. But still, they kept the faith.

Anderson continues, speaking of other martyrs, "With their spiritual vision focused upon Christ, the unseen realities of heaven filled their hearts, as they passed from a world that was not worthy of them to the home that God has prepared for them that love Him."[8] With their lives in jeopardy, they found comfort in Jesus. They kept the faith.

Christian recording artist Dámaris Carbaugh sings about that kind of faith in her signature song, "Christ in Me," describing Jesus Christ as "the hope of glory" and "my shelter from the storm." The chorus ends with this promise:

Should men of evil have their day,
Or should the earth's foundations sway,
None of these can take away the living
Christ in me.[9]

On that cross, Jesus bore the curse of nature and the curse of humanity so that we might be free from the debilitating effects of sin. God's answer to all calamities is the Cross. "Christ has rescued us from the curse pronounced by the law. When he was hung on the cross, he took upon himself the curse for our wrongdoing. For it is written in the Scriptures, 'Cursed is everyone who is hung on a tree'" (Galatians 3:13).

Coping with Doubt

In order to illustrate the demands of keeping the faith in times of great natural disaster, I've paraphrased a parable told by philosopher Basil Mitchell:

In a time of war in an occupied country, a member of the resistance meets a stranger one night who deeply impresses him. They spend the night together in conversation. The stranger affirms that he also is on the side of the resistance—indeed, he is in charge of it. He urges the young partisan to have faith in him—no matter what. The young man is impressed with the stranger and decides to believe in him.

The next day he sees the stranger fight on the side of the resistance, and he says to his friends, "See, the stranger is on our side." The young soldier's faith is vindicated.

But the following day the stranger is in the uniform of a policeman handing members of the resistance to the occupying power—to the enemy!

The young man's friends murmur against him, insisting that the stranger could not be on their side, because he was seen helping the enemy. But the young partisan is undeterred, believing in the stranger no matter what.

Sometimes he requests help from the stranger and receives it; sometimes he asks for help and does not receive it. In times of such discouragement he affirms, "The stranger knows best."

This ambiguous behavior on the part of the stranger causes the young man's friends to ridicule his faith saying, "If that's what you mean by being on our side, the sooner he goes over to the other side the better!" Now the young man faces a dilemma: Does he conclude that the stranger is not on his side after all, or does he go on believing, no matter what?[10]

I believe we can learn the following lessons from this parable that will help us cope with our doubts.

Know Christ

In order to keep the faith when we're prone to doubt God and His goodness, we need to know Christ—deeply, truly, wholeheartedly. If, when we see Jesus, we see God close to us, God loving us, God forgiving our sin, then we will be able to keep believing even though we do not have a final answer to the question of suffering. The better we know Him, the more likely we are to keep trusting Him, even when His actions are confusing and it appears He is not on our side.

In order to keep the faith when we're prone to doubt God and His goodness, we need to know Christ—deeply, truly, wholeheartedly.

To quote Stackhouse once more, "We can respond properly to evil in our lives because *we know that God is all-good and all-powerful because we know Jesus*" (italics added).[11]

Evil of all kinds is a problem for which God's plan of salvation is the solution. Through the Incarnation (the union of divinity and humanity), Jesus is a participant in our suffering, not a distant observer. God is not far from us, uncaring, unthinking, and disconnected. We have the confidence that God will eventually make right His fallen creation. We should not affirm God's control over nature separately from God's final triumph over this world and over history itself. We must believe that both facts are true.

Yes, ultimately the strength of our faith will be dependent on the one in whom we have come to trust. And we can face the uncertainty and trials of life with optimism, helping others along the way. As a *Christianity Today* editorial after the December 2004 tsunami said, "We can . . . know Jesus, and in his embrace, we can in turn embrace the suffering world and offer it a sure hope."[12]

Trust His Promises

When God seems distant during times of great difficulty, we ought not judge His love for us by our circumstances but by His promises:

> I am convinced that nothing can ever separate us
> from God's love. Neither death nor life, neither
> angels nor demons, neither our fears for today nor
> our worries about tomorrow—not even the powers
> of hell can separate us from God's love. No power
> in the sky above or in the earth below—indeed,
> nothing in all creation will ever be able to separate us
> from the love of God that is revealed in Christ Jesus
> our Lord.
> ROMANS 8:38-39

Those of us who have come to know Jesus Christ as Lord are apt to believe His words of hope and comfort. To His disciples, who were about to be left on their own when He returned to heaven and who themselves would later die for their faith, Jesus gave this assurance: "Don't let your hearts be troubled. Trust in God, and trust also in me. There is more than enough room in my Father's home. If this were not so, would I have told you that I am going to prepare a place for you? When everything is ready, I will come and get you, so that you will always be with me where I am. And you know the way to where I am going" (John 14:1-4).

Questions about the mystery of evil are not solved in this life but may be in the next. You'll recall in the parable about the stranger that on some days it appeared as if the stranger was on the side of the enemy and the conflict dragged on without resolution. But remember that God has all of eternity to explain to us (if He should so desire) the mystery of His ways.

That is why we never give up. Though our bodies
are dying, our spirits are being renewed every day.
For our present troubles are small and won't last
very long. Yet they produce for us a glory that vastly
outweighs them and will last forever! So we don't
look at the troubles we can see now; rather, we fix
our gaze on things that cannot be seen. For the
things we see now will soon be gone, but the things
we cannot see will last forever.

2 CORINTHIANS 4:16-18

Trust His Love

Why doesn't our heavenly Father care for us as a good earthly father would—responding to our requests and shielding us from the plagues of this fallen world? The answer is that our heavenly Father loves us *more* than our earthly fathers could possibly love us, but He has a different set of priorities. We value health, and so does our heavenly Father; but He values our faith even more. He delights in providing food for us, but He delights even more when we trust Him—though we are hungry and even starving to death. And yes, He delights when we trust Him even when He seems to be absent when we need Him the most.

> *We value health, and so does our heavenly Father; but He values our faith even more.*

If I may quote C. S. Lewis once more, here he imagines Screwtape saying to Wormwood, "Do not be deceived, Wormwood. Our cause is never more in danger than when a human, no longer desiring, but still intending, to do our Enemy's will [God's will], looks round upon a universe from which every trace of Him seems to have vanished, and asks why he has been forsaken, and still obeys."[13] The demons have no recourse and are indeed astounded when, even without a trace of God in the world and even without evidence of God's care and love, we still obey!

What if God wanted to set up a series of circumstances to prove that some people will go on trusting Him even in the midst of pain and in the absence of clear explanations? What if our faith means so much to the Almighty that He is willing that we suffer if only to prove our devotion even when circumstances seem contrary to His love and care?

What if . . . indeed!

Trust His Plan

The children weeping on CNN after they had lost their parents in an earthquake—that is not the last chapter in the history of this world. Skeptics are unconvinced, but those of us who have met Jesus Christ know that He both knows and cares. We understand that the last chapters of the book He is writing will someday clarify the meaning of the earlier smudged paragraphs.

You might remember the story about a blotch of black paint that was spilled randomly on a canvas. A creative artist decided to paint a beautiful landscape working the black paint into the picture. What appeared to be destructive became part of a larger, more perfect design. In a similar manner, God will see to it that every injustice will be answered, all suffering will be redeemed, and His glory will be displayed for all to see.

After John the Baptist was thrown into prison, he began to have second thoughts as to whether or not Christ was the Messiah. For one thing, the Old Testament predicted that when the Messiah came, the prisoners would be freed (Isaiah 61:1). John made the same error as those who believe God is obligated to make everything right today: he misinterpreted the timing and application of some of God's promises.

As long as John sat in the dungeon, it seemed that Christ was reneging on the promises of Isaiah. And I'm sure John reflected on how unfair it was that he who had played such a vital part in Christ's earthly ministry should find himself imprisoned. So John sent a delegation to Christ to pointedly ask, "Are You the Expected One, or shall we look for someone else?" (Matthew 11:3, NASB). He was polite, but he was hurting badly. Jesus had disappointed him.

In response, Jesus reminded John that miracles were being done and then added, "And blessed is he who does not take offense at Me" (v. 6, NASB). We could paraphrase this verse, "Blessed is the person who is not upset with the way I run My business."

Blessed is the person who does not say, "After the suffering I saw as a result of an earthquake, I will never believe in God again." Blessed is the person who does not say, "I am never going to trust God because He did not keep me from injustice and suffering."

Instead, blessed is the person who understands that he must trust God's heart when he cannot understand His hand. Blessed is the person who knows that he must stand in awe in the presence of the mystery of God's purposes. Blessed is the person who keeps on believing no matter what.

Of all the images that come to mind when I think back to the devastating earthquake in Haiti that killed nearly 200,000 people, the most striking is that of a young mother being interviewed with a baby in her arms.

"I lost my son . . . he died in the rubble."

"Did you get to bury him?"

"No, no chance; his body was crushed in the rubble; I just had to throw him away."

Just then I noticed the camera zero in on her backpack as she prepared to board a bus. Stuffed in a side pocket was a Bible. Then, as she boarded the bus and speaking to no one in particular, she said, "God is our refuge and strength, an ever-present help in trouble . . ." Her voice trailed off as she disappeared from view.

When the report was over, I just kept staring at the TV for a moment, pushing back tears and letting what I'd just seen sink into my soul. A dead child, a baby in her arms, boarding a bus that was going she knew not where; no chance to plan a funeral and pay respects to her precious little one, and there she was, still believing, still trusting that God is her refuge and strength.

Faith in adversity!

This mother—God bless her—began quoting Psalm 46, which was written as a praise song in the midst of disaster. "God is our refuge and strength, an ever-present help in trouble. Therefore we will not fear, though the earth give way and the mountains fall into the heart of the sea, though its waters roar and foam and the mountains quake with their surging" (Psalm 46:1-3, NIV).

Blessed is the person who lets God be God.

QUESTIONS FOR DISCUSSION

1. Do you believe that God is worthy of your trust? Why or why not?

2. What would you do if you had God's powers—and wisdom—for twenty-four hours?

3. Are there times when you have doubted either the existence or goodness of God? Discuss.

4. Why is it that when life seems most unstable, people often turn to God for comfort?

WHAT DO WE SAY WHEN FRIENDS ASK?

*Yet what we suffer now is nothing compared
to the glory he will reveal to us later.*

ROMANS 8:18

WHAT DO WE say when our friends ask about God's role in natural disasters? Some ask because they are seekers, weighing the merits of the Christian faith. Others are believers, but the magnitude of horrific suffering makes them wonder where God was when it was happening or whether He cares.

Let's begin by pointing out that we all are asking the same questions, and we do not have a list of ready answers, slickly packaged and ready for distribution. Intuitively, we know there are no pat answers or glib comments that will convince everyone. Yet questions will come and we need to be ready.

So what *do* we say?

We Must Grieve

We must begin any discussion of tragedy by grieving for those who are in pain. Many of us are better at trying to explain natural disasters than we are at weeping over them. An entire book of the Old Testament describes in vivid detail the grief that the prophet Jeremiah experienced after the city of Jerusalem was invaded and destroyed by the Babylonians. The Bible makes it clear that this judgment on the city, and indeed the entire nation, had been a long time coming. God had warned of coming judgments and sent His prophets to try to get the people to turn from their wicked ways—to no avail. Finally, God's promised heavy hand of judgment fell. But it's likely that some God-fearing, faithful people were killed or starved to death in the siege. Jeremiah recognized that even when the cruel Babylonians came, God was in charge. It was God who inflicted the judgment, but the prophet still wept, just as we should.

Jeremiah writes as though the city herself is speaking:

> Does it mean nothing to you, all you who pass by?
> Look around and see if there is any suffering like
> mine, which the LORD brought on me when he
> erupted in fierce anger. He has sent fire from heaven
> that burns in my bones. He has placed a trap in my
> path and turned me back. He has left me devastated,
> racked with sickness all day long. . . .
> For all these things I weep; tears flow down my
> cheeks. No one is here to comfort me; any who

might encourage me are far away. My children have
no future, for the enemy has conquered us.

LAMENTATIONS 1:12-13, 16

Jeremiah models for us a blending of human compassion
and solid theology. Yes, *God* brought judgment upon His
people by using an evil nation to destroy Jerusalem. But the
prophet is not angry with the Almighty, nor does he stoi-
cally accept suffering because it was deserved. He grieves over
the ruined city. He laments that the
people were so disobedient that they
invited punishment.

Natural disasters cause us to pause,
they cause us to ask hard questions,
and if we care about the world, they
drive us to tears. Can anyone staring at the destruction caused
by a tsunami not weep? Surely a heart of human compassion
identifies with the loss, the suffering, and the hopelessness of
fellow human beings. We should not approach disasters with
an accusatory finger or a detached attitude. Grieving hearts
can only be touched by other grieving hearts—sharing pain
and mingling tears.

Any answer must begin with personal compassion and a
heavy heart.

Tears should lead to deeds—works of service that help
alleviate human suffering. The church is called to reach out
to the world, and nowhere is that more necessary than when
tragedy strikes. Some believers suffer because they are caught
in the tragedy itself; others suffer because they are willing to

Grieving hearts can only be touched by other grieving hearts—sharing pain and mingling tears.

sacrifice in order to help those in need. I commend those who are willing to leave the comforts of home in order to bring hope and healing to the victims. Not everyone can go, but we can all give; we can all participate in helping relief agencies as they serve those who are so utterly destitute. When disaster strikes, the church should be the church!

As she surveyed the repairs done on her home by relief workers, one survivor of Hurricane Katrina commented, "If it weren't for the Christians, we would have no hope here in the Gulf Coast. We needed them, and they showed up." What better witness to the hurting people in this world than to minister to their physical needs first? God wants us to release our grip on our money, our resources, and our selfishness. When disasters come, we should be the first to respond with sacrifice and generosity.

We begin with grief, and then we seek for understanding.

We Must Give Thanks

We must remember that natural disasters are an intensification of what is happening every day in our world—people are constantly dying of starvation, smaller-scale disasters, accidents, and disease. The fact that we are alive is a reminder of God's goodness. We are living on a cursed earth. Death will take us all at one time or another. Because of sin, this planet is not a safe place, nor is it the *final* place.

Natural disasters should remind us of all the blessings we take for granted; they should lead us to deep and lasting gratitude. Before we ask why so many die in natural disasters, we should ask a different question: "Why are so many people—ourselves included—*still living*?" We've learned that sunshine and crops are signs of God's mercy and that disasters reflect His justice and even anger. Yet how many people give Him thanks for beautiful weather and the numerous benefits that nature regularly bestows upon this planet?

Every day that we live with sunshine, food, and health, we are enjoying gifts God does not have to give us. The sun shines to warm us, the rain falls to bless us, and the stars shine to remind us that God is not only in heaven but also on earth to give us mercies we do not deserve. We should be grateful for the times when the earth is firm, when the tornadoes do not blow, and when the floods do not come. The book of Lamentations, which describes Jeremiah's grief over God's judgment on his nation, says, "The faithful love of the LORD never ends! His mercies never cease. Great is his faithfulness; his mercies begin afresh each morning" (Lamentations 3:22-23).

Before we ask why so many die in natural disasters, we should ask a different question: "Why are so many people—ourselves included—still living?"

Life is a gift, and God has the right to give it and take it. We cannot approach this question with an attitude of entitlement, believing that we have the right to life, liberty, and happiness—despite what America's Declaration of Independence says. We can pursue these things, but thanks to our sins and those of our ancestors, God is not obligated to give us the blessings He graciously chooses to send our way.

Often the same people who ask where God was after a disaster thanklessly refuse to worship and honor Him in times of peace and calmness. They disregard God in good times, yet think He is obligated to provide help when bad times come. They believe the God they dishonor when they are well should heal them when they are sick, the God they ignore when they are wealthy should rescue them from impending poverty, and the God they refuse to worship when the earth is still should rescue them when it begins to shake.

We must admit that God owes us nothing. Before we charge God with not caring, we must thank Him for those times when His care is very evident. We are ever surrounded by undeserved blessings. Even in His silence, He blesses us.

Beyond that, of course, is the fact that we will never know what disasters He averted, which ones He did *not* allow to happen, which ones He stopped in their tracks so that, in His mercy, people were not hurt.

We Must Choose

Let's tell our friends that natural disasters force us to decide how we will respond to God. We can either become angry or choose to stand in awe of the Almighty. We can accuse Him or we can worship Him, but neutrality will be difficult, if not impossible.

That is the dilemma that Job faced when his children died in a windstorm. When news reached him of the lightning and the high winds, he did not know the prologue to the Bible book that bears his name and tells his story. He did not know that Satan and God had had a dialogue and that he had been singled out for a special trial. Without explanation, without knowing the fine print of God's purposes, lightning killed all of Job's cattle and a powerful wind (likely a tornado) killed his children.

Satan told God that if Job had his possessions taken from him, he would "curse" God to His face (Job 1:11). Interestingly, scholars tell us that the word *barak* in Hebrew can mean either bless or curse, depending on the context.

Natural disasters force us to decide how we will respond to God.

Although his wife, overcome with sorrow, encouraged Job to turn against God—"curse God and die" (2:9)—Job would have no part of it. With the keen insight of a theologian, he corrected her. "Should we accept only good things from the hand of God and never anything bad?" (2:10). Job knew that both the shining sun and the powerful lightning came from God.

With ten fresh graves on the side of a hill, Job chose to bless and not curse. In response to God, he worshiped:

> I came naked from my mother's womb, and I will be naked when I leave. The LORD gave me what I had, and the LORD has taken it away. Praise the name of the LORD!
>
> JOB 1:21

The next day, things went from bad to worse. By now Satan had permission from God to smite Job with "terrible boils from head to foot" (Job 2:7). Again Job had to choose: should he worship God or curse Him? Again he chose the path of worship and proved *it is possible to worship God even when He does not give explanations for the bad things that happen.*

Natural disasters might drive some people away from God, but for others it has the opposite effect, driving them into the arms of Jesus. The destruction of nature has helped them distinguish the temporary from the permanent. Disasters remind those of us who are living that tomorrow is uncertain, so we must prepare for eternity today. Today is the accepted time; "today is the day of salvation" (2 Corinthians 6:2).

When disasters come, God is not on trial; we are.

We Must Find Firm Ground

Finally, we come to the one clear lesson that natural disasters teach us: even the things that appear solid will someday quake beneath our feet. We must remind our friends to find firm ground while they can.

I talked to a man who survived an earthquake. He said that those ten seconds seemed like an eternity because he did not know when they would end and where he would be when it was over. He ran out onto the street because he was afraid that his house would not withstand the shock. In that moment, what he wanted more than anything was firm ground.

The Bible instructs us to make sure that our lives are built upon a foundation that will never be shaken, a foundation that is not subject to the unpredictable forces of nature.

The Bible instructs us to make sure that our lives are built upon a foundation that will never be shaken, a foundation that is not subject to the unpredictable forces of nature. The upheavals of nature make us realize that we should not put our faith in what is uncertain and will not last, that everything will eventually be destroyed. Earthquakes and tsunamis sometimes represent the voice of God shouting to an unrepentant planet.

The first recorded earthquake in the Bible occurred when God gave the law at Mount Sinai. Let's put ourselves in the trembling sandals of the Israelites:

> All of Mount Sinai was covered with smoke because
> the LORD had descended on it in the form of fire.
> The smoke billowed into the sky like smoke from a
> brick kiln, and the whole mountain shook violently.
> As the blast of the ram's horn grew louder and
> louder, Moses spoke, and God thundered his reply.
>
> EXODUS 19:18-19

I believe the mountain trembled because God wanted the people to stand in awe of His power and to be appropriately afraid to approach Him carelessly. The voice of words spelled out the content of God's moral law; the voice of nature spelled out God's power and authority. The Ten Commandments shouted His rules for living; the trembling of nature shouted His rules for worshiping. To fear Him was not only appropriate but commanded.

Now let's fast-forward through the centuries and consider the earthquake that coincided with Jesus' death: "At that moment the curtain in the sanctuary of the Temple was torn in two, from top to bottom. The earth shook, rocks split apart" (Matthew 27:51).

The timing of the earthquake at Sinai and the earthquake at Calvary could not have been more precise. Two earthquakes, two acts of revelation, and two judgments. On Mount Sinai, God spoke the law with its inflexible demands and warned of the consequences of disobedience; on Calvary, God spoke words of kindness and mercy through the lips of Jesus, even while He was judged for our sins. Both events were accompanied by the shaking of the earth, a reminder that when God speaks, the mountains and rocks tremble.

These two events are given an interesting interpretation in the book of Hebrews. The writer makes a contrast between the old covenant where God shook the earth at Sinai and the new covenant that was instituted at Calvary. In this new covenant, God is seen as speaking from heaven. Let's let the writer describe it:

> Be careful that you do not refuse to listen to the One who is speaking. For if the people of Israel did not escape when they refused to listen to Moses, the earthly messenger, we will certainly not escape if we reject the One who speaks to us from heaven! When God spoke from Mount Sinai his voice shook the earth, but now he makes another promise: "Once again I will shake not only the earth but the heavens also." This means that all of creation will be shaken and removed, so that only unshakable things will remain.
>
> HEBREWS 12:25-27

There are three "shakings" of the earth that are very important. The first was at Sinai, the second was at Calvary, and the third is yet to come. The worst natural disaster of all time is still in the future! Everything that can be shaken will be shaken so that only the unshakable will remain.

And now the conclusion:

> Since we are receiving a Kingdom that is unshakable, let us be thankful and please God by worshiping him with holy fear and awe. *For our God is a devouring fire.*
>
> HEBREWS 12:28-29 (ITALICS ADDED)

The final natural disaster will split the world into two separate kingdoms: the unshakable Kingdom of God and the disintegrating kingdom of the damned.

Natural disasters shake not just the earth, but also our confidence that the earth will go on forever and that our place in it is under our control. Earthquakes and hurricanes vividly remind us that life is short and that the triumph of God over this world is certain. There is a time coming when everything that has been nailed down will be torn up. And in the final judgment, the whole earth will be destroyed and re-created by God. Only what is eternal will remain. Tragedies teach us to hold on to Christ tightly and to everything else loosely.

In the final judgment, the whole earth will be destroyed and re-created by God. Only what is eternal will remain.

Yes, natural disasters are God's megaphone, shouting to this world. But that is not the only way God speaks to us. You may recall that Elijah the prophet was asked to stand on a mountain in the presence of the almighty Lord as He passed by. We read:

> As Elijah stood there, the LORD passed by, and a mighty windstorm hit the mountain. It was such a terrible blast that the rocks were torn loose, but the LORD was not in the wind. After the wind there was an earthquake, but the LORD was not in the earthquake. And after the earthquake there was a fire, but the LORD was not in the fire. *And after the fire there was the sound of a gentle whisper.*
> 1 KINGS 19:11-12 (ITALICS ADDED)

Sometimes God shouts and sometimes He whispers. If we are quiet, we can hear His voice asking us to turn from our own self-absorption to Him. To turn from the uncertainties of this life to the certainty of the next. To exchange our own petty kingdoms for a Kingdom that will endure forever.

If He will not be heard in natural disasters, perhaps God will be heard in the quietness of our souls. Perhaps we will take the time to ponder His mercy and heed the warnings He has given, through Jesus Christ our Lord.

So you, too, must keep watch! For you don't know what day your Lord is coming. Understand this: If a homeowner knew exactly when a burglar was coming, he would keep watch and not permit his house to be broken into. You also must be ready all the time, for the Son of Man will come when least expected.

MATTHEW 24:42-44

Blessed are those who realize that the uncertainties of this life are a reminder to prepare for the certainties to come.

QUESTIONS FOR DISCUSSION

1. Where do you find firm ground when the world around you seems shaken to the core?

2. What do you say to friends who wonder about God's role in natural disasters?

3. When disaster strikes, is your first inclination to bless or curse God? Why?

READY FOR THE BIG ONE

Anyone who listens to my teaching and follows it is wise,
like a person who builds a house on solid rock. Though the rain
comes in torrents and the floodwaters rise and the winds beat
against that house, it won't collapse because it is built on bedrock.

MATTHEW 7:24-25

ALMOST EVERY TIME I visit California, someone is talking about earthquakes. Many residents are expecting "the big one" that could destroy most of Los Angeles and the surrounding areas. For years, geologists have known that the San Andreas Fault, which runs near the coast, is vulnerable to a massive earthquake that could dwarf all others experienced so far.

But the really "big one" will not be confined to California—it will encompass the whole earth. When Christ comes to wrap up history as we know it, the earth and everything in it will be destroyed. This earth, cursed as it is by sin, will burn with fire, and God will remake it according to His specifications.

In the last chapter, we discussed the shaking of the earth, but another passage in the New Testament says the universe itself will disappear, destroyed in a giant inferno. Nothing we have ever seen will compare with it:

> But the day of the Lord will come as unexpectedly as a thief. Then the heavens will pass away with a terrible noise, and the very elements themselves will disappear in fire, and the earth and everything on it will be found to deserve judgment. Since everything around us is going to be destroyed like this, what holy and godly lives you should live, looking forward to the day of God and hurrying it along. On that day, he will set the heavens on fire, and the elements will melt away in the flames. But we are looking forward to the new heavens and new earth he has promised, a world filled with God's righteousness.
>
> 2 PETER 3:10-13

The conclusion follows:

> And so, dear friends, while you are waiting for these things to happen, make every effort to be found living peaceful lives that are pure and blameless in his sight.
>
> 2 PETER 3:14

In the final destruction of the cosmos, all that will remain is God, angels, and God's people. Quite a reminder of what is really important! Of course, the present earth will be re-created and eternity will officially begin (Revelation 21:1).

The question before us is simple: how do we escape the penalty given out at the final judgment? It makes little difference whether we are alive when Christ comes or whether we die and He returns decades later. In one way or another, we will all participate in the end-times scenario. Attendance at the final judgment is mandatory.

If you are wise, you will be prepared for "the big one."

Avoiding the Final Curse

Here is the good news: this world is in trouble, but Jesus came to rescue us from its final consequences. "The Scriptures declare that we are all prisoners of sin, so we receive God's promise of freedom only by believing in Jesus Christ" (Galatians 3:22).

> *This world is in trouble, but Jesus came to rescue us from its final consequences.*

We are all prisoners of sin! What a vivid description of our planet with its suffering, sin, and death. But Jesus came to remove the Curse for those who believe in Him. Let me quote this verse once more:

> Christ has rescued us from the curse pronounced by the law. When he was hung on the cross, he took upon himself the curse for our wrongdoing. For it is written in the Scriptures, "Cursed is everyone who is hung on a tree." Through Christ Jesus, God has blessed the Gentiles with the same blessing he promised to Abraham, so that we who are believers might receive the promised Holy Spirit through faith.
>
> GALATIANS 3:13-14

Jesus bore the Last Judgment for all who believe in Him. When we receive Him as our sin-bearer, we are given the gift of His righteousness so that we can be welcomed into God's presence as if we had never sinned. But only Jesus is qualified to prepare us for eternity because He was not just a teacher, but a *Savior*.

Back in the days when homesteaders were on the prairies, they would frequently light fires around their homes at times when the wind was favorable, burning an area of ground around the perimeter of their houses. When a subsequent prairie fire came toward them, the burned ground would act as a barrier, stopping the fire for lack of fuel. When these pioneers burned the grass and weeds around their homes, they knew they were safe because *they were living where the fire had already been.*

The same is true when we transfer our trust to Jesus. We are standing where the fire of God's judgment has already come. "Anyone who believes in God's Son has eternal life. Anyone who doesn't obey the Son will never experience eternal life but remains under God's angry judgment" (John 3:36). As we learned in chapter six, our God is a devouring fire. In Jesus, however, we learn that God is not distant and remote when we suffer. In Jesus, God suffered that He might redeem us from the final suffering of hell.

In Jesus, God suffered that He might redeem us from the final suffering of hell.

We all remember the images of refugees in places where disaster has hit. People look frantic, lost, shell-shocked. They need food and shelter. These people are a metaphor of our own lives. We, too, are searching for a new beginning. We are all trekking as best we can, en route to our final destination. What we need is a refuge, somewhere that is safe, somewhere that guarantees us a future with God in heaven.

The sons of Korah invite us to run to God for safety when the earth begins to shake. They knew that *God is the only refuge for refugees.*

God is our refuge and strength, always ready to help in times of trouble. So we will not fear when earthquakes come and the mountains crumble into the sea. Let the oceans roar and foam. Let the mountains tremble as the waters surge!

A river brings joy to the city of our God, the sacred home of the Most High. God dwells in that city; it cannot be destroyed. From the very break of day, God will protect it. The nations are in chaos, and their kingdoms crumble! God's voice thunders, and the earth melts! The LORD of Heaven's Armies is here among us; the God of Israel is our fortress.

Come, see the glorious works of the LORD: See how he brings destruction upon the world. He causes wars to end throughout the earth. He breaks the bow and snaps the spear; he burns the shields with fire.

"Be still, and know that I am God! I will be honored by every nation. I will be honored throughout the world."

The LORD of Heaven's Armies is here among us;
the God of Israel is our fortress.

PSALM 46

A Prayer

Father in heaven, I confess the mystery of Your ways. I do not understand Your long-term agenda, nor can I fathom the hidden purposes You have in the pain and suffering experienced by the people You created. Yet I do know that I am a sinner, judged in many different ways for my sin. I thank You that Jesus died to remove the Curse, to free me from Your righteous anger about my rebellion. So in this moment, I receive Jesus as my sin-bearer, as the one who died in my place. I affirm this promise for myself: "To all who believed him and accepted him, he gave the right to become children of God. They are reborn—not with a physical birth resulting from human passion or plan, but a birth that comes from God" (John 1:12-13).

Thank You for receiving me, for I pray in Jesus' name, amen.

Notes

CHAPTER 1: DARE WE SEARCH FOR ANSWERS?

1. http://news.yahoo.com/s/ap/20110311/ap_on_re_as/as_japan_earthquake. Last accessed April 30, 2011.

2. http://news.yahoo.com/s/ap/us_severe_weather. Last accessed April 30, 2011.

3. http://www.usatoday.com/weather/tornado/storms/1999/w503toro.htm. Last accessed May 2, 2006.

4. Steve Kastenbaum, "One Year after Haiti Earthquake: Ruble, Recovery and Reconstruction, CNN, January 12, 2011, http://news.blogs.cnn.com /2011/01/12/ one-year-after-haiti-earthquake-rubble-recovery-and-reconstruction.

5. Mary Wisniewski, "Weather Disasters Keep Costing U.S. Billions This Year," Reuters, September 8, 2011. Jeff Masters, "2011 the Most Expensive Year for Natural Disasters in History," *World Weather Post*, July 14, 2011.

6. Susan Neiman, *Evil in Modern Thought* (Princeton, NJ: Princeton University Press, 2002), 142.

7. A. J. Conyers, *The Eclipse of Heaven* (Downers Grove, IL: InterVarsity Press, 1992), 13.

8. Ibid., 13. Quotation is from T. D. Kendrick, *The Lisbon Earthquake* (Philadelphia: Lippincott, 1957), 137.

9. Ibid.

10. William Barclay, *The Letter to the Romans* (Edinburgh, Scotland: The Saint Andrew Press, 1955), 115.

11. Edward Rothstein, "Seeking Justice, of Gods or the Politicians," *New York Times*, September 8, 2005.

CHAPTER 2: IS GOD RESPONSIBLE FOR NATURAL DISASTERS?
1. John Piper, "Whence and Why?" *World Magazine*, September 4, 1999, 33.
2. Doug Gross, "Digital Fundraising Still Pushing Haiti Relief," CNN, January 15, 2010, http://articles.cnn.com/2010-01-15/tech/online.donations.haiti_1_earthquake-haiti-haiti-relief-twitter-and-facebook?_s=PM:TECH.
3. Timothy Lull, ed., *Martin Luther's Basic Theological Writings* (Minneapolis, MN: Augsburg Fortress Publishers, 1989), 744.
4. Ibid., 742.
5. William Cowper, "God Moves in a Mysterious Way," *Cowper's Poems*, ed. Hugh I'Anson Fausset (New York: Everyman's Library, 1966), 188–189.
6. Quoted in Charles Swindoll, *The Mystery of God's Will* (Nashville, TN: Thomas Nelson, 1999), 115.

CHAPTER 3: ARE THERE LESSONS TO BE LEARNED FROM DISASTERS?
1. Kim Barker, "Many Faithful Spared When Mass Relocated," *Chicago Tribune*, January 5, 2005, Sec. 1, 6.
2. Amy Waldman, "Faith Divides the Survivors and It Unites Them Too," *New York Times*, January 12, 2005, http://www.nytimes.com/2005/01/12/international/worldspecial4/12religion.html.
3. "Tornado Victims Seek Comfort in Sunday Services," FoxNews.com, May 1, 2011, http://www.foxnews.com/us/2011/05/01/tornado-victims-seek-comfort-sunday-services. Last accessed May 1, 2011.
4. Max Lucado, "What Katrina Can Teach Us," *Pulpit Helps*, vol. 30, no. 11 (November 2005), 5.
5. Enjoli Francis, Jeremy Hubbard, Leezel Tanglao, and Michael S. James, "Storms, Tornadoes Leave Dozens Dead in Alabama, Mississippi, Georgia and Tennessee," ABC News, April 27, 2011, http://abcnews.go.com/US/massive-tornado-hits-alabama-storms-leave-16-dead/story?id=13465028&page=2.
6. Aleksandr Solzhenitsyn, *The Gulag Archipelago*, volume 1 (New York: HarperCollins, 1973), 168.
7. Dave Miller, "God and Katrina," Apologetics Press, http://www.apologeticspress.org/articles/351.
8. Jill Lawrence, "Behind an Iconic Photo, One Family's Tale of Grief," *USA Today*, November 11–13, 2005, 1, 6A.

CHAPTER 4: ARE DISASTERS THE JUDGMENTS OF GOD?
1. Dennis Behrendt, "Why Does God Allow Calamities?" *The New American*, December 26, 2005, 32.

2. Michael Luo, "Doomsday: The Latest Word If Not the Last," *New York Times*, October 16, 2005.

3. Byron Paulus, *Revival Report*, Life Action Ministries (Fall 2005), 3.

CHAPTER 5: CAN WE STILL TRUST GOD?

1. I'm indebted to J. M. Monsabre for this idea, as quoted in *12,000 Religious Quotations*, ed. Frank Mead (Grand Rapids, MI: Baker Book House, 1989), 179.

2. John Stackhouse, *Can God Be Trusted?: Faith and the Challenge of Evil* (New York: Oxford University Press, 1988), 103.

3. Origen, *On First Principles* (New York: Harper and Row, 1966).

4. C. S. Lewis, *Mere Christianity* (New York: HarperCollins, 1952), 29.

5. Ravi Zacharias, "The Silence of Christmas and the Scream of the Tsunami," *Just Thinking* (Winter 2005), 1.

6. Stackhouse, *Can God Be Trusted?*, 103.

7. Sir Robert Anderson, *The Silence of God* (Grand Rapids, MI: Kregel Publications, 1952), 150–151.

8. Ibid., 152.

9. "Christ in Me," music and lyrics by Marie Armenia, copyright © Penny Hill Publishing.

10. Basil Mitchell, "Theology and Falsification: A Symposium," in *Philosophy of Religion: An Anthology*, eds. Charles Taliaferro and Paul J. Griffiths (Malden, MA: Blackwell Publishing, 2003), 108.

11. Stackhouse, *Can God Be Trusted?*, 104.

12. As quoted in the editorial "Tsunamis and Birth Pangs," *Christianity Today* (February 2005), 28. Found at http://www.christianitytoday.com/ct/2005/002/4.28.html.

13. C. S. Lewis, *Paved with Good Intentions* (New York: HarperCollins, 2005), 38.

About the Author

Erwin W. Lutzer is senior pastor of The Moody Church in Chicago. A graduate of Dallas Theological Seminary and Loyola University, he is the author of numerous books, including the Gold Medallion Award winner *Hitler's Cross* and the bestseller *One Minute After You Die*. He is also a teacher on radio programs heard on more than seven hundred stations throughout the United States and the world, including *Songs in the Night*, *The Moody Church Hour*, and the daily feature *Running to Win*. He and his wife, Rebecca, live in the Chicago area and have three married children and seven grandchildren.